S0-BVO-933

TABLE TENNIS FOR THE 'SEVENTIES

PICTURE 1. *The author, Johnny Leach MBE, was World Singles Champion in 1949 and 1951, and has won countless other singles and doubles titles all over the world. He represented England as a player on 150 occasions, and during the last decade has served as non-playing captain and team manager of England's world championship team.*

In 1955 he inaugurated the News of the World *National Table Tennis Coaching Scheme at Butlin's Holiday Camps which has continued ever since with ever growing success. He is also well-known for his television commentaries, his long running column in the* News of the World, *and his several instructional works for Kaye & Ward Ltd.*

TABLE TENNIS FOR THE 'SEVENTIES

by Johnny L

with 148 ph

Leach

In the last fifty years table tennis has advanced far beyond the parlour *game* from which it originally evolved. We now accept it as a highly athletic and skilful *sport* in its own right. In fact, it is probably the fastest of all ball games, and certainly the most widely played of all family sports.

But merely to play is not enough. Everyone wants to improve his, or her, performance, and this book shows exactly how this can be done in practical terms. The instruction is easy to follow, and suitable for either sex or any age.

Table Tennis for the 'seventies covers the game from A to Z. It has been compiled by Johnny Leach, former world champion and widely acknowledged as a leading authority on all aspects of play. It features, in over 150 illustrations, all the best players of today in action during the last world championships. Every stroke and counter-stroke, in singles and doubles, is fully described and illustrated, with *emphasis on its practical application in match playing*. The reader can see for himself how champions adapt their strokes and compensate for errors when the world championship is in the balance. Knowledge of team captaincy, playing equipment, the laws and their interpretation, umpiring duties, training, fitness and practice are all essentials which this book helps to provide.

The study of these pages, together with conscientious application of the methods recommended, will help a player of any standard to improve his game—and to enjoy doing it!

A. S. BARN
CRANBURY,

First American Edition 1971
A. S. Barnes & Co., Inc.
Cranbury, N.J. 08512

Library of Congress Catalog Card No. 79–156953

ISBN 0 498 07968 6

All orders or enquiries relevant to this title should be sent to the publisher at the above address and not to the printer.

PRINTED IN THE UNITED STATES OF AMERICA

CONTENTS LIST

Chapter One **Introduction**

Claims that table tennis is the fastest-growing sport in the world are not difficult to substantiate. Since 1926 when representatives of seven nations met to form the International Table Tennis Federation, and to entrust England with the running of the first World Championships, one hundred more nations have joined in. Some European countries have a quarter of a million registered players, while in the Far East, where table tennis is included among the leading national sports, the numbers of players are counted in millions.

The organised modern game developed in England from such parlour pastimes as 'Ping Pong', and in this country we have seen the number of authorised leagues grow from a mere 19 in 1927 to the present 300-odd.

The reasons for its popularity are also easily identified. Table tennis is not an elaborate sport. It is played indoors with comparatively inexpensive equipment and it requires only a limited amount of space. It can be enjoyed by all members of the family, offering exercise and entertainment to players of any age or standard, even to the physically handicapped.

Yet played at its best table tennis is probably the fastest ball game that exists. It is an athletic sport in its own right, and also provides a valuable means of training for other sports. It demands quick thinking and instantaneous reaction, and aids the development of these attributes.

It is indeed a truly international sport, played in more countries than any other. My own introduction to the game was typical; I enjoyed innumerable battles against my father across the dining-room table. When in the mid-thirties I first saw the top players of the day in action, great stars like the Hungarian trio of Barna, Bellak and Szabados, I was fired with the urge to emulate them. They displayed skills which finally took the game out of the ping pong era and into the realms of top-class sport.

Play was slower in those days, and not just because of the higher net. It was a pace which lent itself to longer rallies, and a much more stylish stroke play than we now see. Indeed Victor Barna ranks in my estimation as the most elegant stylist of all time as well as the longest reigning champion. At his best he was an all-rounder who depended on clever variation in the amount of backspin he imparted on defensive returns to make openings for his lethal backhand attack. Bo Vana, the Czech who followed Barna as World No 1, had a vicious forehand which he combined with a superb drop shot, the latter showing the delicate touch of a master violinist.

The late Richard Bergmann was the most efficient match-winner I have ever seen. Victor Barna won the world singles title five times. Bergmann only four. But I have no doubt Richard could have improved even on the great Barna's record had his run of success not been interrupted by the war. Bergmann normally based his game on impregnable defence, but could switch his tactics as required.

Of course, up to the Second World War most championships were fought out by about eight outstanding Central European stars, there being no opposition from the Middle and Far Eastern countries. How different today when a player must exhaust most of his mental and physical energy in order to overcome fierce opposition in every round before reaching the last eight of the World Championships.

Table tennis boomed after the war. Many of us had taken up the game for recreation in services canteens during the emergency with no means of measuring how good we were. I was a 'nobody' when I went into the RAF. It came as a big surprise to me when I emerged to find myself ranked as England's No 1 player. Others similarly found they had reached international, or at least good club standard, and welcomed the chance 'civvie street' offered them to display their skills. It would be conceited of me to imagine that the standard of play in the 1949 World Singles Championship, which I won, was any higher than those held immediately before the war. The game simply started again from where it left off in 1939, though improvement was fast because of the greatly increased number of participants. My own all-round style was based on defence.

I won the title again in 1951, in Vienna, then came the Asian invasion. Apart from the all-European championships of 1953 in Bucharest, the Japanese stars completely dominated the world honours throughout the rest of the 1950s with their revolutionary sponge rubber bats, and superfast, forehand hitting in penhold-style.

Then in 1961, in Peking, the Chinese came on the scene to master the Japanese as thoroughly as the Japanese had mastered the Europeans. The Chinese had developed a method of hitting the ball very hard indeed, using a very short back-swing, which made it very difficult for opponents to anticipate the direction of their shots. The Chinese also produced superior services, using complicated wrist movements to accentuate spin. They liked to dictate matters from a close-to-the-table position.

Table tennis is, of course, a major sport in China, and their top players work and train much harder for success than those in any other country. They achieved the highest standard the game has yet seen, but in 1965 withdrew from world competition because of their cultural revolution. The honours returned to Japan, then in 1971, with China competing again, the men's singles crown returned to Europe through Stellan Bengtsson of Sweden. However, no country has yet achieved a standard higher than that of the Chinese champions in 1964.

At the start of the seventies the emphasis is still very much on attack, but the hit-or-miss phase which followed the introduction of sponge bats in the 1950s is over. Ball control had been achieved at a much greater speed, and the rallies are getting longer. The sandwich bat has been mastered.

In my time, if a player gained a 5- or 6-point lead he had virtually won the game. In the last few years half a dozen points have meant nothing, they could be recovered so quickly. In the future we can expect less and less unforced errors, more subtle all-round play and tactics, in fact a gradual return to the attractive style of the late 1930s–except that the pace will be very much greater.

So the champion of tomorrow will not only need a superb all-round technique, but a standard of fitness much higher than ever before.

Add the following basic requirements, which I consider essential:

1. Natural ability for games with a moving ball
2. Character, which embraces determination, intestinal fortitude; dedication to practice and training
3. Mastery of all the strokes and counters, and the ability to string them together in sound tactical combination
4. Flair, or that extra quality that enables you to develop and employ successfully at least one outstanding feature of your game.

Chapter Two **Equipment**

While table tennis is economical in its demands on playing space and equipment, there are minimum standards which must be met if really skilful play is to be achieved. Inadequate space, and second-best conditions and equipment, can be harmful.

The basic needs are a large room, a properly constructed table and suitable lighting.

The standard table is 274 cm (9 ft) long by 152·5 cm (5 ft) wide. It should be supported so that its playing surface lies in a horizontal plane 76 cm (2 ft 6 ins) from the floor.

The table can be made of any material, providing it yields a uniform bounce of not less than 22 cm (8 ins) and not more than 25 cm (9 ins) when a standard ball is dropped from a height of 30·5 cm (12 ins) above its surface.

PICTURE 2. *The full-sized table, with dimensions.*

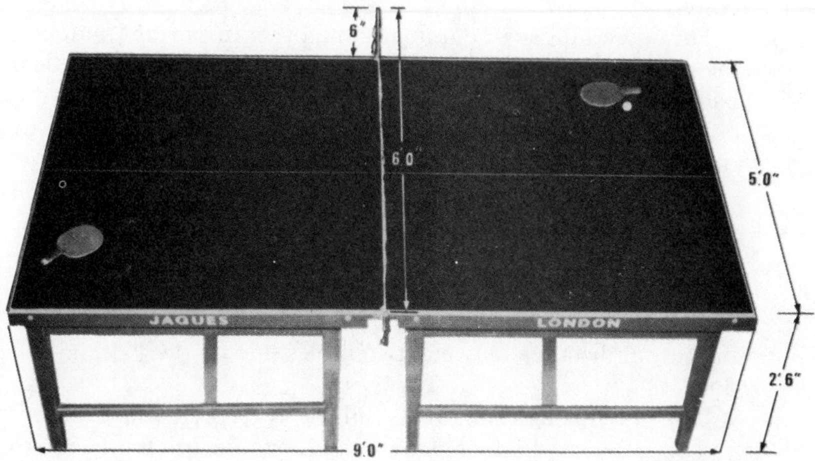

The playing surface must be dark coloured, and matt, with a white line (2 cm–$\frac{3}{4}$ in–broad) along each edge. For doubles play, the playing surface should be divided into halves by a centre line (3 mm broad) and this may be permanently marked.

The dark green net with a white top, which divides the playing surface into two equal courts, is 183 cm (6 ft) in length (measured with its suspension). Throughout its length the upper part of the net must be 15·25 cm (6 ins) above the playing surface. It is suspended by a cord attached at each end to an upright post 15·25 cm (6 ins) high, the outside limits of each post being 15·25 cm outside the side line.

A table of sub-standard size can handicap and discourage a player, but even more important is a correct bounce which is indispensable to good habits of stroke play. This is dependent on correct support, material, thickness and paint surfacing, which you can only be sure of finding in a professionally manufactured tournament table.

For a satisfactory bounce, the top should be of 1 in thick plywood, spray painted with dark green cellulose paint and finished with a matt surface. I cannot recommend a table which is less than $\frac{1}{2}$ in thick as being suitable for serious play.

If you are bound to practice at home on a table of non-regulation size, say only 8 ft long instead of 9, you should lower the net to 5 ins, and so on, in proportion. But the sooner you can transfer your attention to the real game on a full-sized table, the better.

For official tournament finals, and other important matches, the minimum playing area is 46 ft long by 23 ft wide. The ideal background is one of a uniform dark colour. The floor must not be of stone, or linoleum, but of hard, non-slippery wood or thermo-plastic, not white nor brightly-reflecting.

Sprung wood-flooring tends to affect the bounce of the ball off the table. A wooden floor found to be slippery should be washed with warm water.

During early rounds of an official tournament, the minimum run-back from each end of the table should be 12 ft, and the minimum distance between two tables side by side 8 ft, 9 ft for doubles.

The playing area should be defined by dark surrounds about 75 cm (2 ft 6 ins) high. These should be stable, but light enough to fall without injuring a player who runs into them.

Measured at table height the light should be a minimum of 40 foot-candles in strength uniformly over the table, and not less than half the table strength over any part of the playing area. No light may be suspended less than 4 m (9 ft 9 ins) from the ground.

For ordinary club play you should aim to have at least 15 ft of clear space at either end of the table, and 8 ft on either side. The absolute minimum playing area is 28 ft by 15 ft.

The minimum standard of lighting for club play is three 150 watt lamps in 20 ins circular billiards shades, one over the centre of the table, and one over each end. The distance from lamp to lamp should be 5 ft 6 ins and the height from the floor 9 ft. The important thing is that the lighting should be symmetrical so that conditions are identical at both ends.

The ball must be spherical, with a minimum diameter of 37·2 mm ($4\frac{1}{2}$ ins) and maximum of 38·2 mm ($4\frac{3}{4}$ ins). It must be made of celluloid, or a similar plastic, and be white and matt. Its minimum permissible weight is 2·40 gm (37 grains), maximum 2·53 gm (39 grains).

PICTURE 3. *Before starting play in a World Doubles Championship match at Munich in 1969, Dragutin Surbek (Yugoslavia) is shown spinning the ball, presumably to satisfy himself that it is perfectly round.*

This procedure, boring to spectators, and suspect as 'time-wasting gamesmanship', will soon be rendered obsolete by modern methods of ball production and testing, already so perfect there is little likelihood of finding a 'dud' ball.

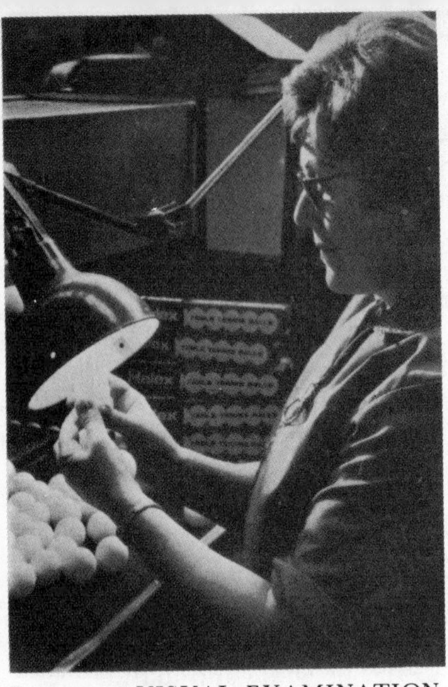

PICTURES 4, 5, 6, 7.
How a Championship Ball is tested.

PICTURE 4. VISUAL EXAMINATION *This is the first of the series of examinations following the actual production process. A team of girls scrutinise every single ball for possible defects. Any that do not reach the high standards set are not passed through for further testing.*

PICTURE 5. BIAS TEST *Following the visual examination, each ball is rolled down an inclined ground plate-glass table, its seam at right angles to the table. This test rejects any balls that may have a bias to one half.*

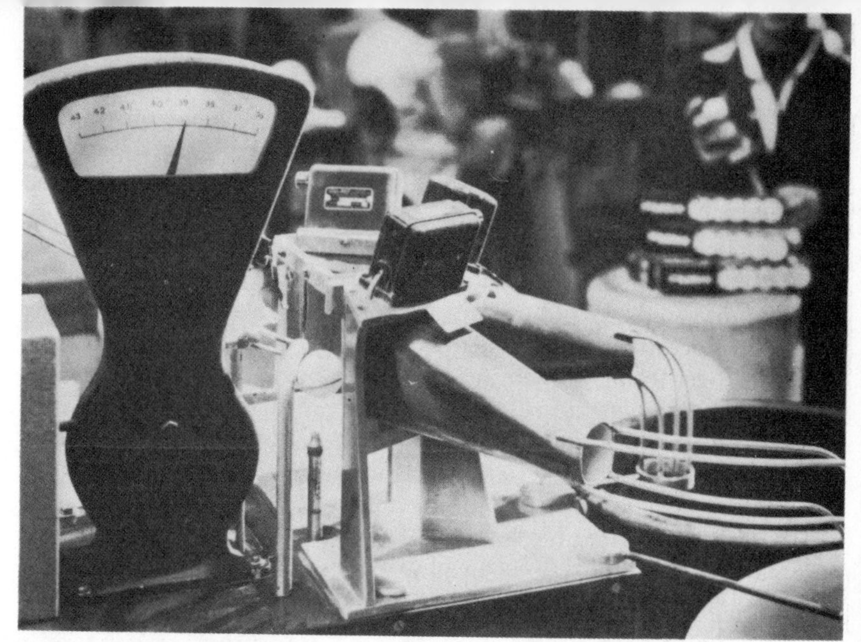

PICTURE 6. WEIGHT *To meet ITTF specifications all balls must weigh between 37 and 39 grains. Each ball is individually and automatically weighed. The machine is so set that any ball falling outside the authorised limits is rejected into a separate container in order to ensure all 3 Star balls meet with the specifications.*

PICTURE 7. HARDNESS *A special gauge has been designed in which a ball is compressed against a spring-loaded plunger. In this way the overall consistency of the material surface can be recorded.*

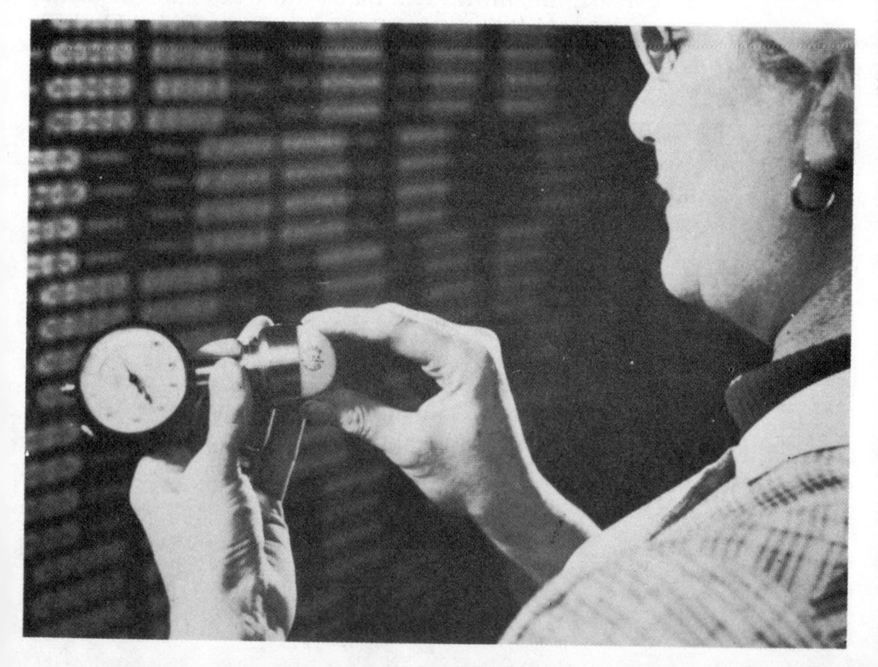

Any ball stamped 'ITTF Official' or 'ITTF Approved', or one bearing the approval stamp of a national association such as 'ETTA Approved', is a guarantee of a ball of good quality.

So far as players' dress regulations are concerned, white or light coloured clothing which might tend to distract an opponent is not allowed. Also, any badge, or lettering on a playing garment must not be so large or conspicuous as to break its uniform dark colour. Breaches of this regulation are normally decided by a Tournament Referee.

I recommend a simple, dark shirt and shorts as best for men, a dark shirt and skirt for women, worn with a good pair of rubber shoes with non-slip soles. Clothes must be comfortable because in play you are called upon to make rapid changes of direction, and they should be smart. Most find that the smarter they look, the smarter they play.

The standard dress for players representing the ETTA is the official shirt with ETTA badge, trousers, shorts or skirts, white socks and white shoes. If a cardigan or pullover is worn it must be the same colour as the shirt. For players chosen to represent England in World and European Championships a royal blue track suit with 'ENGLAND' embodied on the back of the suit is provided by the Association. For Junior players the letter 'J' is included after England.

A table tennis bat may be of any size, shape or weight, and should have a matt finish. The blade must be made of wood, continuous, of even thickness, flat and rigid. If the blade is covered on either side, this covering must be one of the following types:

1. Plain, ordinary pimpled rubber, with pimples outward, of a total maximum thickness of 2 mm
2. Sandwich, with pimples outward, of a total maximum thickness of 4 mm
3. Sandwich, with pimples inward, total thickness 4 mm
4. A combination of any of the above surfaces.

'Sandwich' is a surface consisting of a layer of cellular rubber (known as 'sponge') surfaced by plain, ordinary pimpled rubber.

Your first consideration in choosing a bat should be whether it feels right for weight, and whether you can handle it with easy confidence.

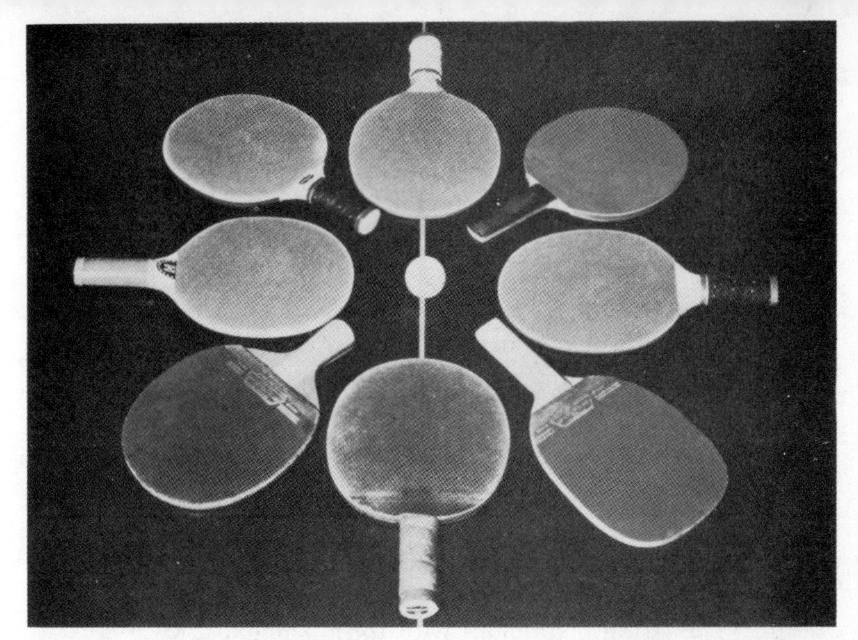

PICTURE 8. *A selection of modern bats of all shapes and sizes. At* bottom centre *is my personal choice. To the left of this is the one-sided penhold bat favoured by the Chinese champions, and to the right is pictured the Japanese penhold bat.*

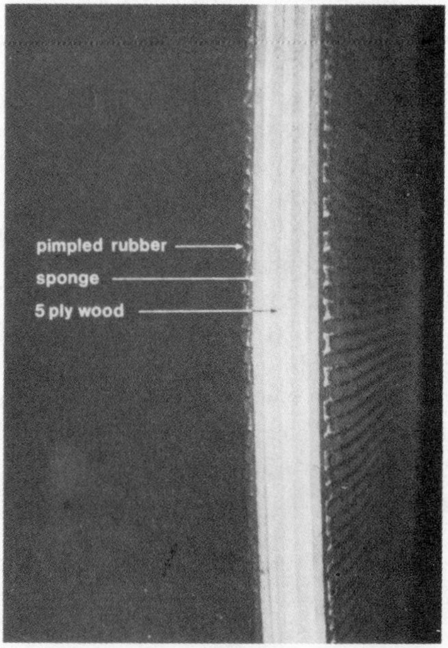

PICTURE 9. *Section of a sandwich bat with pimples 'outward'. Alternate layers of plywood, sponge and pimpled rubber are shown.*

As regards surface, a standard plywood bat with ordinary pimpled rubber on either side is ideal for good ball control and the acquisition of good, all-round stroke play. This is the type I used to win the world championship, and it is still used by quite a few top players today. However, the vast majority of players in the 'seventies are using sandwich bats. Sandwich is rather harder for the beginner to master, but it offers artificial aid to accentuate both the speed and the spin of one's shots. It acts as a cushion in defence, and a catapult in attack.

Sandwich with pimples outward is used for more speed with spin, and this is the type favoured by the majority of top players today. Sandwich with pimples inward is slower, but gives closer control and extra spin.

Several players find it advantageous to use a combination of different surfaces. For example, Ebby Scholer of West Germany, has plain pimpled rubber on the backhand side of his bat, and sandwich with pimples inward on the forehand.

The Asian champions with their penhold grips use extra-light bats with sandwich rubber on one side only. There is nothing but wood on the other side, which is not used.

Each type of bat requires a different technique, or at least adjustment in timing, and each individual must decide which one suits him best. However, it should be emphasised that though it is important to find the bat to suit one's style, the ability of the player will always count for more than the bat he chooses.

The only likely change in equipment during the 'seventies is one of colour. As a result of laboratory research, and practical experiment all over the world, the desirability of substituting a yellow for a white ball has gained considerable support. If the yellow ball should eventually be adopted, a change from white to yellow lines on the table seems likely. It may also prove necessary to alter those instructions regarding dark clothing, background and surrounds. It may prove that a yellow ball can be better seen against a lighter background.

However, it has already been shown that the average player can very quickly adjust to such changes. These should not be in the least detrimental; in fact they could lead to a general improvement in standards of play.

Chapter Three **How to Play Western Style**

The 'shake hands' grip is favoured by the vast majority of players outside Asia, and is ideal for Western-style table tennis.

To find it simply put your bat on the table, pick it up by its blade with your non-playing hand, then grasp the handle with your playing hand as if shaking hands with it.

This is the basic grip. Try playing a few shots to see how it suits you. You should find, like most of us, slight adjustments can improve your production of different shots.

For example, to play forehand shots most players like to have their forefinger extended across the back of the blade to provide

PICTURE 10. *The basic 'shake hands' grip (back view).*

PICTURE 11. *The basic 'shake hands' grip (front view).*

PICTURE 12. *Forehand variation (back view).*

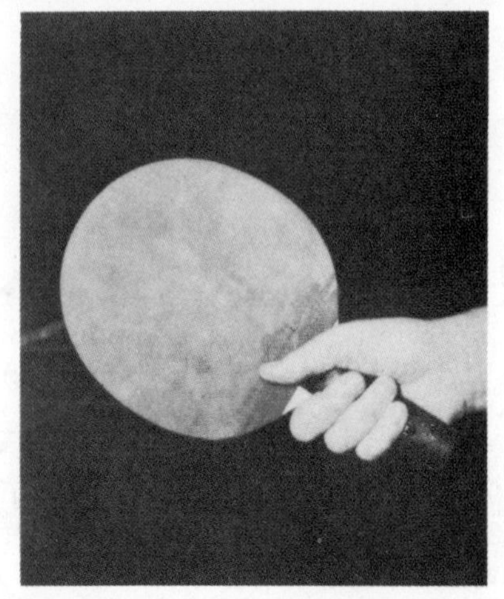

PICTURE 13. *Backhand variation (back view).*

steadiness and better touch (Picture 12). The thumb is tucked out of the way, leaving three fingers curled round the handle.

However, you may be among those who prefer two fingers behind the blade for forehand strokes. If this, or any other modification suits you, then use it. Be comfortable, that's what matters most.

To make backhand strokes, most players reverse the positions of thumb and forefinger. The thumb moves up so it lies down the centre of the blade to give support (Picture 13) while the forefinger drops down near to the edge of the blade to avoid coming into contact with the ball on impact.

If your forehand grip is correct in the first place, you will soon find that the backhand comes naturally and without conscious effort.

Ready Position

The position you adopt to receive service needs careful consideration.

Obviously, it should be one which will lead you quickly and smoothly into the right attitude for your favourite shot. But since your opponent is allowed to serve to any part of your court, your initial position must also guarantee your ability to reach the ball no matter where it may be directed.

Most players who use the orthodox 'shake hands' grip find it best to take up a central position, and this is the neutral base to which they try to return after playing each stroke.

Your attitude should be relaxed and comfortable, yet alert. Feet comfortably spaced, knees slightly bent, you rest on the balls of the feet–prepared for anything.

The distance away from the table to stand is the one which best suits your height and reach. To find this, first take up the attitude described, crouched square to the centre of the table, holding the bat with the playing arm extended downwards and forwards. Now adjust your position in relation to the table until you are just able to touch its edge with the edge of your bat.

Pictures 14, 15 and 16 show typical 'ready positions' of international stars pictured during world championship play. In

PICTURE 14. *Amelin (USSR)–relaxed, yet ready to move rapidly in any required direction.*

PICTURE 15. *Scholer (West Germany). You may think he looks* too *relaxed, but in his case appearances are deceptive. Besides having the best defence in the modern game and a perfect temperament, Scholer has lightning reflexes.*

PICTURE 16. *Alser (Sweden) seems alert to all possibilities as he prepares to receive service from Tan (Cambodia).*

each case the expert is ready to cope with any type of service with just one, simple movement. One step to either side will enable him to cover a service dispatched wide on either forehand or backhand wing. One step forward with the left foot and he will be perfectly placed to deal with a short ball on the forehand. Alternatively, a step forward with his right foot will put him in an equally good position for a backhand return.

By moving the appropriate foot one pace backward, at the same time turning on the opposite heel, he can instantly prepare himself for a defensive return against a deep, fast service down either wing.

The habit of starting from, and returning to the central position between strokes provides a clear perspective at all times.

Stance

The ideal position from which to play nearly every stroke in the book is *sideways-on*, as in all bat-and-ball games.

The right-handed player with the orthodox grip aims whenever possible to have his left shoulder and left leg leading (i.e. nearer to the table) in order to play a forehand stroke. Right foot and right shoulder should lead in order to produce a backhand stroke of maximum power and accuracy.

Both strokes should start with the player nicely balanced on the balls of his feet, his knees slightly bent.

By the way, although the players featured are all experts, you'll notice that the pictures in this book do not all demonstrate perfect stroke production. This is because they were taken in the heat of world championship action, the speed and tactics of which often demand compromise. Indeed, far from being sideways-on, many leading players are seen to play their shots from an almost square-on position.

However, it is most important to note that top players compensate in appropriate ways for these 'short-cuts' they take. For example, they compensate for lack of backswing, and lack of body assistance in any stroke, by pivoting from the hips at the last moment, so simulating the sideways-on movement. Then they exaggerate the vitally important follow through which follows.

Even so, it must be accepted that emergency modifications mean less power, and less margin for error. So when learning, my advice is to try and achieve perfect strokes by using the full sideways-on stance. Modifications can be considered later, by which time you should appreciate what you are sacrificing, and what you must do to make up in other ways for the missing part of a stroke.

Basic principles *do* matter, and for success every liberty taken demands compensation.

Push Strokes

The simple 'push' is the basic stroke. It can safely be used at any time as a counter to any stroke played by an opponent, or when sparring for an opening.

It means merely pushing the ball back across the net, using forehand or backhand as appropriate, yet it is a stroke not to be despised. Correctly played, it is the foundation of nearly all the more attractive strokes.

PICTURE 17. *Gabriele Geissler (East Germany), one of the world's top defensive players, plays a steady, backhand push stroke.*

PICTURE 18. *An inelegant, but effective forehand push stroke used in action by Dragutin Surbek (Yugoslavia). Only a champion could get away with a shot like this!*

PICTURE 19. *Malcolm Sugden (Scotland) produces a very well controlled backhand push during a rally with Mirkasim (India). Note his studied concentration.*

PICTURE 20. *Amelin (Russia) is quite satisfied to use the simple push here to manoeuvre himself into an attacking position against Shifmann (USA).*

Top players practice the 'push' every day, playing backhand and forehand strokes alternately as a means of achieving delicate ball control, also improving their footwork at the same time.

It is most easily played from the sideways-on stance so the body does not impede the stroke. With the forearm horizontal, and the bat tilted slightly back at the top, the bat should be moved steadily forward and slightly downward. You can only learn from experiment and experience to what extent your bat should be tilted to deal with the various spins an opponent might employ.

As the bat moves forward, the weight of the body should be transferred from the back to the front foot. Contact against a return of normal pace is usually made when the ball is level with the body. But you will have to reach well forward for a short

PICTURE 21. *After an exchange of push strokes by Barnes (England) at the far end, and Kohno (Japan), the latter seems ready to pounce. Unless Barnes' return is very short, or very long, Kohno will make a 'killing'.*

return, while a fast ball naturally calls for a later moment of contact.

Always think of the bat as an extension of the playing arm. The aim is to cultivate such control over the light ball you can almost 'feel' it when making contact. It is also important to place your shot shrewdly, or you could be setting yourself up for your opponent's 'kill'. Allowing your movements to follow through to their natural extension after the ball has left the bat is a very important factor in control and accuracy.

If using a sandwich bat you will find it necessary at contact to give the ball a slight 'lift' over the net, then to follow through in a slightly upward plane. With plain, pimpled rubber, however, both your approach and follow through should be on a steady, horizontal line.

Try to achieve a smooth, rhythmic movement. This is im-

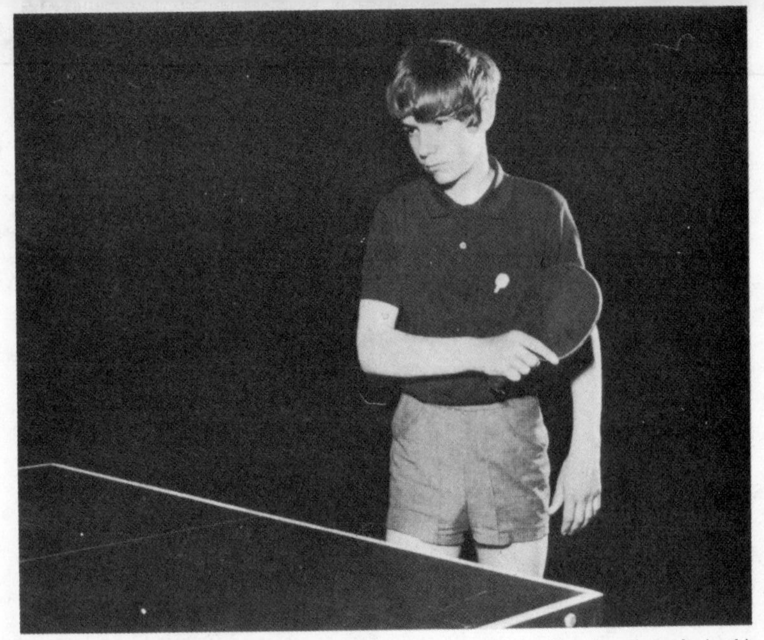

PICTURES 22–24. *Peter Taylor (England) demonstrates the correct backhand push stroke in this sequence which shows (22) approach*

portant in all stroke play. You'll find it much easier if you have placed your feet in the correct sideways-on position an instant before making contact. As soon as the stroke has been completed, return automatically to the mid-table 'ready' position from which you are prepared for the next move.

As well as being correctly placed, your feet must maintain the balance of the body; a shot made off balance is a shot without control.

Practising push strokes from alternate wings, forehand and backhand, is the best way of getting used to moving the feet efficiently into their correct positions.

The ideal stroke at which to aim is demonstrated on the backhand wing by Peter Taylor in Picture sequence 22–24.

(23) moment of contact

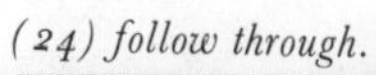

(24) follow through.

Spin

The push stroke does not call for the use of spin, but most of the others do, so before dealing with them you should learn something about backspin, topspin and sidespin.

Look at the diagrams, shown in Picture 25. Charged with backspin a ball will rotate backwards while it is moving forward. Backspin is imparted by bringing the bat down, and *underneath* the ball in a chopping action at the moment of striking. The further underneath the ball the bat strikes, the greater the amount of backspin.

As an illustration, put a ball on the table and hold it there with the top of your forefinger, wrist at rest on the table top. Your finger should be placed just behind the top of the ball. Now press down with your forefinger. The ball, charged with backspin, will spring forward for a few inches, then roll back towards you.

Thus backspin gives the ball a tendency to bounce backwards towards the striker after it has hit the table surface. It is mostly used for defence.

PICTURE 25. *(1) Topspin. The ball is arrowed to show direction of topspin.*
(2) Backspin. The ball is arrowed to show direction of backspin.

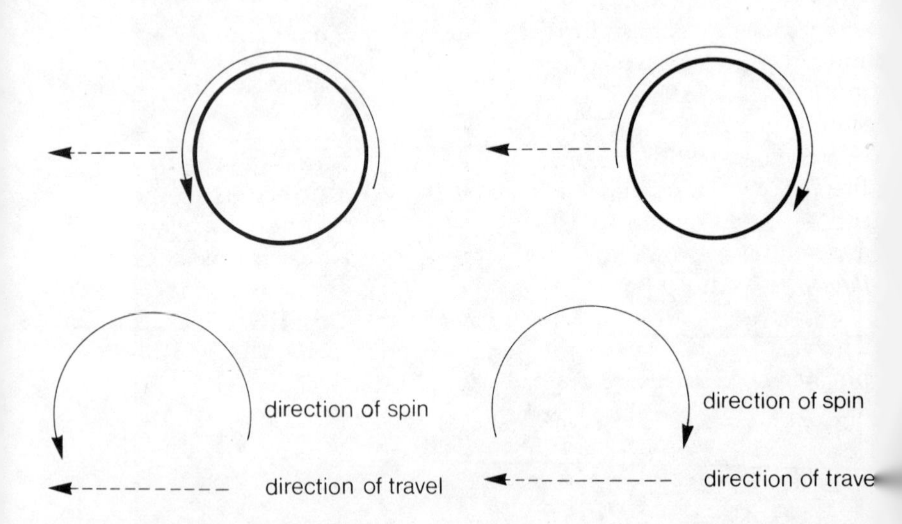

Topspin is the opposite, normally an attacking spin and the main counter to backspin. It makes the ball rotate forwards while it is moving forward, and is produced by brushing the bat upwards and forwards across the top of the ball as it is struck.

A ball carrying topspin has a tendency to dip in flight over the net, then to shoot forward and upward on touching the table surface, before dipping again.

Sidespin makes the ball spin horizontally either to the left or right. It is produced by moving the bat across the ball from one side to the other as it is struck. If struck from right to left, for example, the ball will tend to break to your opponent's left-hand side after touching the table surface.

The sandwich bat has made sidespin a much more reliable and effective weapon than it was once considered. Nowadays it is mostly used in conjunction with either backspin, or topspin.

Since in every case the degree of spin is determined by the length of time the bat remains in contact with the ball, the follow through of strokes becomes particularly important. However, as will be seen, stroke technique must be varied according to the type of bat used.

Service

In modern times, despite strict laws to limit its full advantage, service is a key factor in any game, and it demands special study.

Besides the straightforward topspin and backspin serves, numerous variations are possible. Used imaginatively, with disguise, these can give a player instant supremacy and on occasions even enable him to score a point outright.

However, before trying to 'ace' opponents with your service, first find out what you are allowed to do and get into the habit of serving correctly. To my mind, nothing is worse than sacrificing a potential advantage by serving carelessly or incorrectly, so *throwing* points away.

Service must always be made from the palm of the free hand. The ball must rest on the palm without being cupped or pinched by the fingers, *the latter being held together with thumb free.* The ball must also be visible to the umpire at all times. (See

PICTURE 26. *Surbek (Yugoslavia).*

Pictures 26–28–apparently even the world's leading players sometimes break the Service Law, and in my view the risk they take is not justified.)

Incidentally, any player unable to conform strictly to the service law because of some physical disability should notify the umpire before play begins. The umpire has authority to modify the service law in such cases.

The ball should be tossed into the air from the palm of the free hand, without imparting spin and as nearly vertical as possible. If the ball should veer more than 45 degrees to either side of the vertical the umpire will call a 'fault'.

The ball should not be struck with the bat until it has started to descend from the peak of its trajectory, and the bat's position at the time must be behind the end of the table, or an imaginary continuation of the table.

Service in table tennis is unique in that the ball must first touch the server's side of the table then, passing directly over or around the net, touch the receiver's court before the latter can attempt his return.

Picture 27. *Amelin (USSR).*

Picture 28. *Scholer (West Germany)–See how these international stars begin their services, with the ball placed on the palm of the stationary free hand and clearly visible to the umpire.*

Special Note.
Strictly speaking two of these services, and many others, made during the 1969–70 World Championships, were illegal. As the camera reveals, neither Surbek nor Scholer is holding together the fingers of the hand supporting the ball, as the law requires. Presumably because no advantage was being gained, the umpires concerned ignored this technicality, but don't be tempted to copy this method–you may not be so lucky!

By the way, if the server misses the ball altogether–and this does happen–he loses the point automatically, since the ball was in play from the moment it left his hand. Also, if his bat should slip from his grasp, a stroke made with the hand alone is 'not good'. According to the laws the only 'fair strike' is when a ball is 'hit with the bat, or bat hand below the wrist'.

Within all those requirements there are four basic services to learn, all of which are best made from the appropriate sideways stance. They can of course be varied by speed, angling, and placing, and in this way provide a full range for the average player.

PICTURES 29–31. *In this sequence, Jill Shirley (England) demonstrates the forehand backspin service. Note that contact is made* after *the ball started to drop, as the service law demands.*

The *backspin* service can be made from either forehand (as illustrated by Jill Shirley in Pictures 29–31) or backhand. First take up the appropriate sideways-on stance, bat being held at near shoulder-height with the blade tilted forward at the bottom.

As the ball is tossed into the air from the free hand, the bat is brought forward and downward to strike the descending ball just below its centre. At this moment the ball should normally be a few inches above table level. The follow through is in a forward, and slightly upward direction.

This service is also illustrated in action by left-handed Alan Hydes (Pictures 34 and 35).

The *topspin* service may again be made forehand or backhand from the appropriate sideways stance. The forehand service is demonstrated by Jill Shirley in Pictures 32–33.

Start with the body inclined forward, the bat being held just behind and below the stationary ball, blade of the bat tilted

PICTURES 32–33. *In these two pictures Jill Shirley demonstrates the forehand topspin service (32) just after contact, and (33) the follow through.*

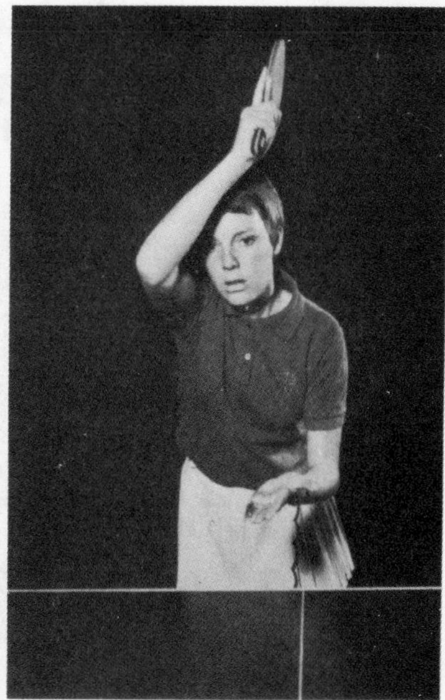

PICTURES 34–35. *A heavy backspin service by left-handed Alan Hydes (England). Note that the ball must be projected near vertically upwards from the palm of the free hand, without imparting spin. The spin comes by chopping the bat down and underneath the falling ball.*

forward. Throw up the ball from the palm of the free hand and, at the same time, move the bat forward and upward. Once the ball has dropped to a few inches above table level, your aim is to move the bat forward and upward to brush the top of the ball.

A fast topspin service, or heavy backspin well placed will often produce the sort of return to put you on the attack. Top Japanese players are able to land very fast topspin services right on the baseline, causing the ball to kick up into an opponent's body.

Always *think* before you put the ball into play. Make sure that you yourself are settled and composed, and that your opponent is ready.

With the sandwich bat, many intricate spin services are possible. Most of these combine sidespin with topspin or backspin, at the moment of striking. They can be very effective when introduced with surprise, but much practice and care is necessary because the margin for error is very small.

Pictures 36 and 37 show an example of the amount of care and effort star players employ in order to produce an effective service.

PICTURE 36. *Ybrashi (United Arab Republic) serving to Alser (Sweden) far side.*

PICTURE 37. *Surbek (Yugoslavia) serving to Orlowski (Czechoslovakia).*

Top players today have developed a wide range of trick services within the laws, and no effort is spared in trying to 'ace' an opponent. By crouching low in this manner a low trajectory, and heavy backspin combined with sidespin, can be achieved.

There are two kinds of sidespin shot. If the bat is drawn across the ball from right to left it will cause the ball to break to the server's right immediately after it has come into contact with the far side of the table.

The alternative, of course, is to cut across the ball from left to right, and this causes the ball to break to the server's left on touching the table.

Either of these breaks can be produced when brushing over the top of the ball for topspin, or when chopping down behind the ball for backspin. But to be successful, all your movements must be smooth and precise. Most players find that their early attempts are fraught with errors. These are usually caused by striking the ball too soon, or too late, or by taking the eye off the ball for an instant. It takes practice, and lots of perseverance.

Defence

I have always advocated learning the defensive strokes first, and still do so despite the modern emphasis on attack. Knowing you have sound defensive strokes to fall back on when necessary gives added confidence; besides which a good grounding in them makes attack easier to learn afterwards.

With the sandwich bat almost any ball can be returned with reasonable safety simply by blocking. The sponge will 'give' on impact, then spring back to boost the speed at which the ball would return from an ordinary hard rubber surface.

However, merely returning the ball safely each time is not what the game is all about. You seek not only to slow down your opponent's attack, but to set him problems as well. For this purpose the backspin, or chop stroke, is ideal.

This can be made forehand or backhand, and once again for maximum effect and power the sideways stance is best in either case. You start with your weight on the back foot, and transfer it to the front foot as your bat makes contact with the ball.

Begin the approach with the bat shoulder-high, aiming to make contact at about waist height when the ball is dropping. Knees and trunk should bend as the arm movement progresses forward and downward. The point of contact is behind, and below the centre of the ball.

During the stroke, your weight should be shifting from your back to your front foot. The bat is then allowed to follow through in an upward curve, finishing near shoulder-height if using the sandwich bat. With an ordinary, pimpled rubber bat the chopping movement should be more directly downward on the ball, the follow through ending at about knee-height.

Forehand and backhand shots are made in a similar manner, but a full and correct sideways-on stance is particularly important to ensure a well-controlled shot on the backhand.

A main secret of good stroke production on either wing is first getting into a good position in which you can play the ball without reaching. Reaching puts you off-balance, upsets accuracy, and it will also make it more difficult to return to the ready position for the next shot.

When opposing a hard hitter who occasionally drops the ball short, you may need to defend closer to the table edge than usual, giving your opponent less time in which to produce his

11
8
Dunlop

5
Dunlop

PICTURES 38, 39, 40. *Backhand defensive returns at the three significant stages of approach, contact, and follow through, by Alser (Sweden).*

Alser is recognised as one of the most perfect stroke players in the modern game, yet the camera reveals that even he has theoretical faults in his technique. He is, for example, leaning back while his bat is going forward in one instance, making it more difficult for himself to get into position for his next shot.

However, Alser usually has a good practical reason for departing from the textbook method. Judging it tactically advisable to play the ball earlier, he is compensating for the ball's extra speed at this point by 'giving' to it as much as he dare.

The textbook method is, after all, only a guide. With commonsense you adapt its lessons to suit each situation.

PICTURES 41–42. *Jill Shirley demonstrates the forehand chop stroke in two stages–(41) contact, and (42) follow through.*

PICTURES 43–45. *Jill Shirley's immaculate backhand chop, showing (43) approach, (44) contact and (45) follow through.*

PICTURE 46. *Caught out of position, Alser makes a fine recovery with this long-range forehand chop return. By exaggerating his follow through he is able to compensate for the fact that he was falling back while making his stroke.*

strokes. The best stance for this type of game is with the body angled at about 45 degrees from the table. A right-handed player would have his left foot nearer the table on the forehand wing, or his right foot nearer on the backhand.

A quick switch from forehand to backhand is then best made with a jump, there being insufficient time to move each foot separately.

Played from close in, the ball will be moving faster than usual and heavier backspin will be necessary with the bat tilted back more. The wrist can be brought into play, turning the bat under the ball as contact is made. A good example of this stroke played in action is Pictures 47–50 featuring Borzsei of Hungary.

Go for *length* with your chop shots. A return to mid-table, no matter how severe the backspin, can be classed as 'a gift' to most opponents today.

PICTURES 47–50. *Note the tremendous concentration of Borzsei (Hungary) in making this fore-hand chop return; also his full knees-bend in the follow through, head still well down though the ball is already winging its way over the net charged with heavy backspin.*

After learning the chop strokes under ideal conditions you will find that in matchplay such conditions rarely apply. But experience teaches you how to adapt; how to get as close to textbook perfection as the situation allows.

A useful variation of the backspin shot is the float, or 'dummy chop'. For this, a normal chop stroke action is employed up to the moment of contact. At this point, however, instead of cutting underneath the ball with the bat you *ease off*, before continuing with the normal follow through.

If you are able to deceive your opponent with your action he will approach the ball as if it were carrying backspin to the normal degree. In fact it will be carrying scarcely any backspin, so the unwary receiver is likely to put his own shot well beyond the far edge of the table.

As an alternative to chop defence, the Asian stars have developed long-range counter-topspin drives which are difficult to handle. Several Western players have also armed themselves with this valuable, additional weapon, but the 'chop' remains the principal means of defence.

PICTURE 51. *Making this forehand chop slightly in front of his body, Scholer (West Germany) still looks as perfectly balanced and composed as ever. No wonder he ranks as the most consistent defensive player in the game.*

PICTURE 52. *Miko (Czechoslovakia) addresses himself perfectly for the chop stroke. Note his nice balance.*

PICTURE 53. *A backhand chop return by Judy Williams (England) during world championship play.*

Attack

Topspin

The main attacking stroke is the topspin drive. It can be made from either forehand or backhand, ideally again from the appropriate sideways stance with the weight starting on the back foot and being transferred to the front foot during the action.

For the forehand stroke, the arm movement starts from a position behind the body, with the bat held at about waist height. Point of contact should be when the ball has reached a position approximately level with your body, by which time your bat should be a little above waist height, tilted slightly forward at the top of the blade.

PICTURE 54. *A forehand topspin drive perfectly executed by Hans Alser (Sweden) in play against Tan (Cambodia).*

PICTURE 55. *See how Pauline Piddock (England) gets power into this forehand drive, her full weight coming forward on to a bent left knee. In this game, Pauline gave a superb all-round performance to defeat the (then) reigning world champion, Morisawa of Japan.*

PICTURE 56–57. *Experienced Leah Neuberger (USA) plays her immaculate forehand topspin drive against Miss Jacks (Ghana). Note Leah's sideways stance, her weight starting on the back foot and being transferred to the front foot during the action.*

PICTURE 58. *A typical Denis Neale forehand topspin drive during a counter-hitting duel with the 1967 World Champion, Hasegawa (Japan). Note that both players have their feet wide apart, a not uncommon sight today when the speed of exchanges allows time for only one foot to be moved into position for each stroke. This foot may then be quickly, and easily recovered to a central position ready for the next stroke.*

PICTURE 59. *Amelin (USSR) plays a forehand drive from his own backhand wing to Shifmann (USA). Most forehand attackers now find themselves hitting in similar manner, from backhand court to backhand court, most of the time. As a consequence, tacticians should note, it is often down his forehand side that a strong forehand hitter proves most vulnerable.*

PICTURES 60–61. *In two separate shots, Gomozkov (USSR) is seen shaping for, then following through from a forehand topspin drive. Picture 60 shows him admirably poised and concentrating intently for a perfect shot. His finish in Picture 61 is not quite so good, as he is leaning slightly backwards instead of coming forwards, and thus losing power. No doubt he was caught out for once by the speed of his opponent, Cordas (Yugoslavia).*

PICTURES 62–63. *It always amazes me how a big man like Dragutin Surbek (Yugoslavia) can move with such agility and grace to produce such great shots. In Picture 62 his weight is on the ball of his left foot, his right heel being used for balance. Clearly he is watching the ball like a hawk.*

In Picture 63 Surbek has both feet off the ground, having put 100 per cent effort into his drive, which is faced by Orlowski (Czechoslovakia).

PICTURE 64. *Left-handed Alan Hydes (England) follows through after counter-hitting at long range, an effective shot even though he has been forced to play it on the retreat, and is therefore seen leaning back, instead of forward as he should be at this stage.*

The playing arm is then moved forward and upward, the bat brushing the top of the ball to impart topspin, then continuing to the full, natural extension of its follow through which is near head-height in front of the body.

Having begun at right-angles to the net, the shoulders are turned by the body movement so that they finish almost parallel with the net.

The tilt of your bat, and your wrist movement, must be adjusted to suit the speed and type of spin employed by your opponent, but this can only be determined by experience. In time the adjustment becomes almost instinctive.

The backhand movements are very similar to the forehand, feet positions being reversed. However, contact is normally made a little earlier than for the forehand and, since less turn of the trunk is involved, the wrist may be turned on contact to give the topspin imparted an extra boost. If the latter is still further exaggerated it is possible to make a last-second change in the direction of your shot, as illustrated in several pictures.

PICTURE 65. *Caught square on, Alser (Sweden) is about to play a topspin defensive return on his backhand. Lacking speed, or power, his shot must rely on its accuracy.*

PICTURE 66. *A fine backhand topspin positional shot by Amelin (USSR), who has changed the direction of his shot at the last moment by turning his wrist over. Kohno (Japan) looks to be completely out-positioned, but like most Japanese stars he is amazingly agile, so Amelin must be prepared at once to turn round in anticipation of Kohno leaping across and making a fast diagonal return wide of his forehand. The Japanese are masters of this surprise tactic.*

PICTURE 67. *Mrs Amelin plays a change-of-direction backhand similar to her husband's, with much more chance of success since the feet of her opponent, Miss Sabuncuoglu (Turkey), seem rooted to the spot.*

PICTURES 68, 69. *In play against Kohno (Japan), England's Chester Barnes uses his very accurate topspin backhand shots to control a fast rally and move the Japanese star rapidly from side to side.*

PICTURE 70. *Pauline Piddock (England) used her backhand stroke most effectively in the defeat of the 1967 World Champion, Morisawa (Japan), one of the big 'shock' results of the 1969 World Championships.*

PICTURE 71. *Vladimir Miko (Czechoslovakia) specialises in sudden changes of direction like this with both his backhand, and his forehand topspin shots. He looks as if he might have fooled his opponent, Lewin (Sweden), on this occasion.*

PICTURE 72. *A backhand drive which went wrong! Kjell Johansson (Sweden) is famed for the fluency of his forehand, but if he has a weakness in his game it is this, his less reliable backhand.*

PICTURE 73. *Alan Hydes (England) has a very accurate and consistent backhand shot, but it lacks power–and this picture shows why. Typically Alan is reaching for the ball, and playing the ball over his body. But his sacrifice of power for convenience is deliberate. It enables him the more readily to move into his favoured forehand stance.*

Most players favour forehand as opposed to backhand strokes and, since it is scarcely possible to give equal attention to both at match-play speed, the use of a modified sideways stance for the backhand is popular, also sensible because it enables you to introduce your more powerful forehand more readily.

You will see from the pictures of world stars in action that very few adopt the full sideways-on stance for the backhand stroke, but stand at an angle of about 45 degrees with the end of the table. Their shot is played towards the front of the body, hips pivoting to transfer the weight forward.

Of course, players realise they cannot get as much speed and power into their stroke as from the full sideways-on stance, but they are willing to sacrifice this for convenience. When the chance comes to switch to the forehand stance, all that is necessary is to pivot on the front foot, carrying the body weight at that stage, then turn the back foot until it places the player in the sideways-on stance for his forehand stroke.

It is extremely important to compensate for the short-cut taken with the backhand stroke by exaggerating the follow through, continuing the movement of the arm and bat so that the bat stays in contact with the ball for the maximum possible time. This aids power, control and accuracy.

Don't try to hit the cover off the ball at first. Begin playing the shot slowly, without much spin, regarding it as an extension of the push stroke. Then gradually start building up speed until you develop a really effective point-winning stroke.

A useful tactical weapon is the 'dummy' topspin shot, which begins and ends as for normal topspin. At the moment of contact with the ball, however, the brushing action is *eased-off* so that the ball is returned with little or no new spin. Since it will still be carrying some of the topspin originally imparted by the opponent, however, the ball will be rotating backwards as it crosses the net. If the opponent treats your return as a normal topspin drive he will play the ball downwards instead of upwards, and so almost certainly play it into the net.

Drop Shot

Deadly, but difficult to master, the drop shot is a short return placed only an inch or so the other side of the net where it bounces very little either forward or upward. To be successful, the shot must be well disguised, and used only when the opponent is far away from the table–otherwise it could provide a 'gift' for one's opponent to kill.

A 'feather' touch is required so that the ball barely creeps over the net.

Ideally it should be played from the sideways stance, either forehand or backhand, though the former is preferred by most exponents. The knees should be slightly bent, body and arms relaxed. Start a swing as if to make a topspin drive, but, instead of taking the ball at the top of its bounce, relax the grip at this point, slide the bat under the ball almost horizontally, and lift the ball sufficiently upwards to carry it clear of the net.

It should be played over the table, the nearer to the net the better.

Kjell Johansson is known as one of the best exponents of this shot in the modern game.

PICTURE 74. *A perfect drop shot by Kjell Johansson, following a series of hard-hit forehands to drive his opponent farther and farther back, until no longer visible in our picture. Then, having received a short backspin return, Kjell shaped for a further drive but, at the last moment before contact, he arrested the forward motion of his bat, slid it quickly underneath the ball and lifted the ball gently just over the net.*

The Kill

The kill is a flat hit made, without imparting spin, against a ball above net height. It succeeds by sheer power, combined when possible with accurate placing out of the reach of one's opponent. No reply is expected.

The sideways stance should be used, and the bat should be brought flat against the ball at the peak of its bounce, then moved straight towards the target point.

Players today take a calculated risk by employing the kill at the slightest opportunity. To be able to kill with certainty is a vital skill which must be mastered.

PICTURE 75. *A full-blooded 'kill' by Denis Neale (England) which carries sufficient power to pierce Hasegawa's defence, even though the Japanese star seems well positioned to cover it.*

Half-volley

The half-volley is normally played on the backhand. It is little more than a block, with contact being made immediately the ball has bounced. There is very little approach movement of arm and bat, and little follow through movement is necessary. It can be played either sideways-on, or from a square-on position.

With the plain, pimpled rubber bat the half-volley was once regarded merely as an emergency shot to gain time in which to recover position. However, the sandwich bat has given it added significance.

With sandwich it is only necessary to put the bat in the path of the ball and the sponge surface will automatically accentuate the speed at which the ball returns over the net. So, used at the right moment, well placed and boosted by a slight push, the half-volley has become a valuable attacking stroke with which to out-manoeuvre an opponent, and even spreadeagle him on occasions. It also remains a very useful defensive shot, since one needs only to reach the ball and block it in order to stay in the rally with a chance.

PICTURE 76. *Ebby Scholer (West Germany) plays a shrewd, short half-volley during the heat of a rally.*

PICTURE 77. *A sudden, point winning half-volley by Chester Barnes (England) skilfully angled short on Kohno's (Japan) backhand side.*

Though the arm movements necessary are very slight, the half-volley should be smoothly played for accuracy, and of course the bat must be tilted to suit the spin and speed employed by the opponent. To meet topspin the bat should be tilted forward; against backspin it should be tilted backward.

The Loop

The loop is a heavily accentuated topspin drive which has now become a basic stroke in its own right.

When first introduced into the game by the Japanese in the 1950s it created havoc among players unfamiliar with its vicious spin which causes the ball to kick, or skid violently after bouncing.

Then players learnt to deal with it by adjusting the timing of their returns. It was found that the loop must either be taken very early, perhaps with a half-volley, before the spin can take

PICTURES 78–79. *Amelin (USSR) plays the high loop by bringing his bat vertically upwards and, while so doing, brushing the top of the ball very severely. On bouncing in his opponent's court, the ball will kick violently.*

PICTURES 80–81. *An excellent example of the loop produced with maximum topspin by Karl Bernhardt (Sweden) opposing Chu Chang Sook (Republic of Korea).*

PICTURE 82–84. *A sequence showing the low loop stroke of left-handed Alan Hydes (England), a shot he introduces brilliantly as a variation of his normal fast, attacking shots.*

full effect; or very late, with a long-range chop, after most of the spin has died away.

Even when combined with sidespin, the loop is now seldom an outright point-winner in top-class championship play, but it remains an extremely valuable variation which will often force a loose return.

The first type of loop was the high loop, now widely used against slow backspin returns. For this, the bat is brought vertically upward, finishing high above the head. At precisely the right moment during its passage, the bat brushes the back of the ball very severely. This stroke needs a great deal of practice to get the timing right, and it is not uncommon even for senior players to miss the ball altogether when attempting the stroke.

When correctly executed the high loop stroke will cause the ball to lift some three or four feet over the net; then, on bouncing, to kick off the table.

0
0
0
0
2
Dunlop

0
0
1
1
2
2
Dunlop

PICTURES 85–86. *Compare the follow through of Brian Wright (England)–85, and Hans Alser (Sweden)–86. The latter has added sidespin to his loop shot, and this will cause the ball to break to his opponent's left hand side as well as kicking violently.*

The main difference of the low loop, which can conveniently be added as a variation to normal topspin attacking shots, is that the path taken by the bat is more forward than upward. A larger area of the ball is brushed on contact, and though the amount of spin is less than with the high loop, the resultant speed of the ball is greater.

A further variation is the dummy loop, for which one pretends to make a normal high loop but, at the moment of contact, greatly modifies the brushing action. The follow through is then continued high above the head. Played in this manner the ball will cross the net at the expected height, but should the opponent treat it as a normal loop, allowing for a much greater degree of 'kick' than it actually carries, his return will almost certainly end up in the net.

The Chop Smash

The chop smash, a kill made by bringing the bat down, and forcibly forward against a high ball at the peak of its bounce, has been rendered virtually obsolete by the loop and the improved flat hit. If used, however, heavy sidespin should be combined with the backspin so the ball will skid away on bouncing, and one's target area should be the centre of the table to allow ample margin for error.

Chapter Four How to Play Asian Style

The Penhold Grip

Because of the penhold grip employed, permitting the use of only one side of the bat, Asian style is virtually 'one-stroke table tennis' with the emphasis on all-out forehand attack. This is made possible by exceptionally nimble footwork.

You take hold of the bat by wrapping forefinger and thumb around the base of the handle so that they rest comfortably on the rubber-covered blade. The three remaining fingers are spread at a comfortable distance apart on the wooden side of the bat. The latter give support and help control.

Picture 87. *The penhold grip (front view), natural grip for the majority of Asians. All strokes are played on this side of the bat.*

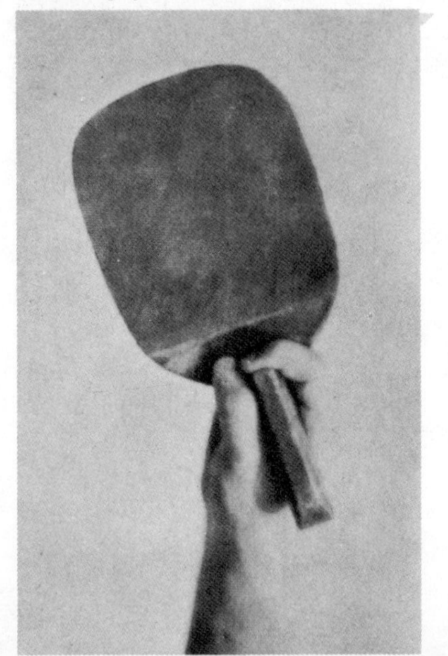

Picture 88. *Penhold grip, as seen from behind the player, three fingers supporting on the wooden side of the bat.*

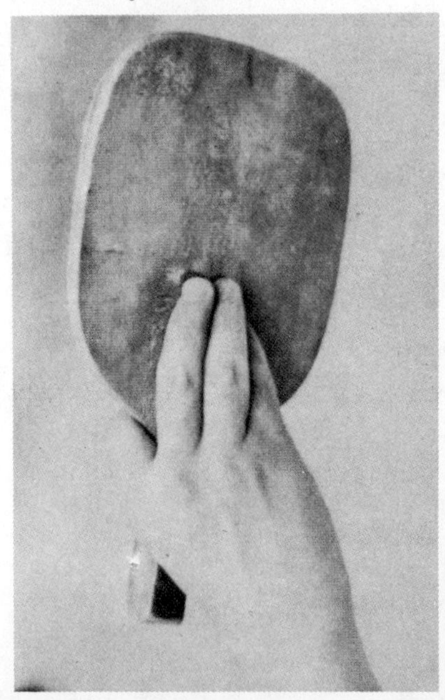

With this grip the bat becomes a natural extension of the playing arm for forehand strokes. Topspin forehand drives and loops can be produced in a similar manner to those made with the 'shake hands' grip and, it would seem, with even closer control. However, there can be no backhand stroke as we know it. To play a shot on his backhand wing the penholder must either move very quickly across to adopt the forehand stance, play an emergency half-volley, or develop the rare and difficult technique of a few Chinese champions like Chuang-Tse-Tung who, in the 1960s, amazed the table tennis world by unleashing the powerful backhand drive most of us thought impossible for the penholder.

Chuang-Tse-Tung and his colleagues turn their bat to the left and, by holding it above wrist level, are able to give the ball a tremendous slap, equivalent in power to a full-blooded Western backhand drive.

However, so far only a few have been able to master this freak shot, and the majority of Asian style exponents accept the limitation of a very cramped backhand, planning their tactics accordingly. Their ready position is normally a pronounced

PICTURE 89. *The Asian ready position, wide of the backhand court, shown here by Lee Dal Joon (USA).*

PICTURE 90. *Another illustration of the Asian ready position. Ito (Japan) is ready to receive a backhand service from Alex Rosmarin (Belgium).*

crouch on the toes outside the table on their backhand side. This leaves a large portion of the table exposed, but by fast footwork top exponents somehow manage to cover the whole area without difficulty and also, usually, quickly take the offensive.

The Asian penholders have managed to introduce into the game an astonishing range of intricate spin services, largely by imparting side- as well as top-spin as their bats strike the ball. However, their greatest skill is the ability to *disguise* the type and direction of the services they use, and the penhold grip definitely seems to offer them an advantage for this deception.

For variation, many Asian stars can produce a very fast top-spin service which they place accurately on the opponent's baseline. This is very difficult to return with safety.

PICTURE 91. *A tricky service by Kohno (Japan), combining backspin and sidespin. His opponent is Jimmy Langan (Ireland).*

PICTURE 92. *Lal Dal Joon (USA) prepares to serve penhold in the correct manner, ball resting on the palm of his free hand.*

PICTURES 93 and 94. *A heavily chopped forehand service, made from his backhand wing by Kohno (Japan).*

Most Asiatics scorn defence; when attacked they counter-attack. But some, like Miss Hamada of Japan, have successfully adopted the 'shake hands' grip and orthodox Western style, just as European players like Zoya Rudnova (USSR) have mastered the penhold grip and Asian style.

Miss Rudnova enjoys a great deal of success against both European and Asiatic opposition. Her penhold-style may look less smooth and fluent than that of some Japanese champions, but it is nevertheless most effective.

In the West we maintain there is far more scope for stroke play with our natural grip which enables one to use both sides of the bat. However, by holding their bat like a chopstick the Asians have proved that their natural grip has advantages of its own. Grip really is just a matter of personal preference.

PICTURE 95. *Miss Hamada (Japan), one of the few Asians who uses the Western 'shake hands' grip, shapes for a forehand defensive chop.*

PICTURES 96, 97. *Miss Hamada makes an orthodox, Western backhand chop.*

PICTURES 98, 99, 100. *Zoya Rudnova, the penhold-style expert from the USSR, has forced her opponent right away from the table. She now places a forehand topspin drive just over the net on the backhand court to clinch the point.*

PICTURE 101, 102, 103. *A good illustration of the tremendously fluent and powerful topspin forehand drive of a Japanese star. Unlike the Chinese, most Japanese players use a full backswing as well as a full follow through. Tasaka, shown here, plays his shot with feet rather closer together than usual, though in fact it is one the Japanese seem able to produce from almost any position or stance.*

For the last twenty years the Asians have dominated world championship table tennis, but not because their grip and style are superior. The main reasons for their success are that they have been fitter, faster and more dedicated than any of their rivals.

Any Westerner who feels that he has the aptitude for penhold-style will now be encouraged by his own national coaches to try and develop it. Being 'different' could offer you a decided advantage. At the same time, Western-style opponents always welcome practice against the penholder's less familiar technique and tactics.

With penhold style, slick footwork becomes more essential than ever since the exponent must move around the table to use his effective forehand stroke at all times. An all-out attacking policy is also necessary, since the penholder's defence is limited to push-strokes, half-volleys, or blocks. If forced away from the table edge he must retrieve the ball with long, topspin loops.

PICTURE 104. *Whether using the penhold, or Western grip, the Asian stars put all they've got into a 'kill'. Typically, Miss Hamada makes a full knees bend in her follow through, ensuring maximum power and control.*

Opposing the Penholder

Speed alone will not beat the Asian-style champion. In fact Westerners always have difficulty in matching him in this department. We cannot out-hit him, so our aim must be to outwit him tactically, moving him continually in and out from the net, and from side to side of the table.

The penholder usually stands on his extreme backhand wing to receive service, intent on using his forehand stroke no matter what. You might place your service wide down his forehand, and the next shot wide down his backhand. To vary this, introduce a very short chop shot just over the net. This is often difficult for him to deal with, because the average penholder likes to start his swing from below the table edge.

Probably the most effective weapon is a strong backhand. See how Chester Barnes used his against Kohno in the 1969 World Championships to outmanoeuvre his Japanese opponent.

PICTURE 105. *Kohno makes a forehand drive down Barnes' backhand wing.*

PICTURE 106. *Barnes returns the ball wide down Kohno's forehand wing forcing him to leap across and make an emergency shot. A simple block wide down Kohno's backhand should now win the point for Barnes.*

PICTURE 107. *Barnes is again shown controlling the rally with his backhand. A penholder normally plays the majority of his shots down an opponent's backhand wing, which suits Chester Barnes admirably.*

PICTURE 108. *Barnes has again caught Kohno out of position, this time with an angled forehand drive to Kohno's backhand.*

PICTURE 109. *Langan makes a short return wide on Kohno's forehand court.*

A left-handed Westerner with a strong forehand, like Jimmy Langan (Ireland), is also well-equipped to deal with the right-handed penholder. Langan is also a very clever tactician.

PICTURE 110. *Making use of the speed on the ball from Kohno's forehand, Langan plays an angled backhand return to try and catch Kohno out of position.*

PICTURES 111, 112. *Here we see Denis Neale (England) in action against former world champion Hasegawa (Japan), who plays the hard-hitting Asian game using a semi-Western grip. In Picture 112 Neale is seen sparring for an opening, controlling the rally with his backhand. In Picture 111 Neale has played a backhand from an almost square-on position, which means his shot can have little power or speed, while Hasegawa is in a perfect position to leap in with a forehand smash.*

In this case the marks for tactics must go to the Asian star.

Chapter Five **Doubles**

Good teamwork is vital in doubles play, since the ball must be struck by each of the four players in turn. In other words, after you have struck the ball, it is your partner who must make the return.

In addition, space is very limited, so close understanding, and an agreed system whereby each player will leave the table clear for his partner to make the next shot, are essential.

What all doubles players try to avoid is returning to the same position from which they started their stroke. To do so would mean obscuring one's partner's view of the ball.

A left-hander partnering a right-handed player can be the ideal combination, since each can play his strongest stroke without having to run round his partner. If both partners are right-handed, it is advantageous for one to have a strong forehand, the other a strong backhand.

There are several different systems used by partners to avoid each other during play. One is for each partner to move back and to one side after completing his stroke, leaving the whole table space clear for his advancing partner. Another is for one partner to circle behind the other after making each shot. But where partners favour backhand and forehand respectively, each can conveniently take one half of the table as his base.

Experienced doubles pairs switch automatically from one system to another to suit circumstances. Some achieve an almost telepathic understanding.

The thing to remember is to try and induce an opponent to return the sort of ball your partner will relish. You play to your partner's strength, as well as to your opponents' weaknesses.

To keep out of your partner's way the use of the full sideways-on stance for your strokes, as well as fast and sure footwork, makes your task easier. It is obviously a further advantage to be able to play shots in a confined space with the minimum movement.

A strong forehand player would normally take up a central position in order to serve, or receive service, while his partner, stronger on the backhand wing, would wait behind him and to his right.

When the strong backhand player is serving or receiving, he would normally stand outside the right-hand corner while his partner waits on his left.

If players decide to take half the table each, the server or receiver will be nearer the table so, after making his shot, he must move back and to the right to give his partner full freedom.

Apart from complementing each other in playing style, it is obviously desirable that the partners should suit each other in temperament. Great doubles pairs not only have an uncanny understanding, they somehow seem able to compensate for each other's temporary faults and weaknesses. When one is not in peak form, the other partner will often succeed in raising his own standard of play to meet the occasion.

Generally speaking, an attacking policy pays off best in doubles. When making a series of attacking strokes, a sound basic plan is to direct the ball straight back towards the opponent who has just returned it to you, remembering that he must get out of the way before his partner can attempt his stroke.

PICTURE 113. *The basic 'ready position' for doubles play, shown by 1969–70 World Champion Ito and his Mixed Doubles partner, Miss Kowada (Japan).*

Note: *The Japanese pair assume the more pronounced crouch. Obviously they intend to go straight into the attack under any circumstances.*

PICTURE 114. *Karenza Matthews and Mary Wright (England).*

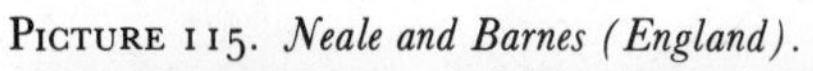

PICTURE 115. *Neale and Barnes (England).*

PICTURE 116. *Denis Neale is about to make a backhand service. This will enable him to move quickly to one side, and so leave the whole table free for his partner, Chester Barnes, to play forehand.*

While the latter shot is being played, Neale will move round behind Barnes, ready to move forward to make his own return. The rally will continue with the English pair moving clockwise round each other.

PICTURE 117. *This time it is Barnes who is about to make the backhand serve, the more easily to leave the whole table free for Neale's very strong forehand.*

PICTURES 118–122. *This shows a sequence of play during the world doubles championship match Barnes and Neale (England)–v–Andersson and Neiderf (Sweden).*
PICTURE 118. *A good forehand by Neale, now starting to move back as Barnes moves in.*

PICTURE 119. *Barnes follows up with a well-placed backhand, his object being to force a suitable for Neale's powerful forehand kill.*

PICTURE 120. *Neale goes in for the 'kill'. However, Andersson succeeded in returning this smash with a block wide down the Barnes forehand side.*

PICTURE 121. *Barnes plays a shrewd forehand. He is also ready to leap clear.*

PICTURE 122. *An accurate backhand return from Neale leaves the Swedish pair hopelessly out of position. Point to England!*

PICTURE 123. *Whatever stroke you play in doubles, your partner must take the return, so it is important for him at all times to know what type of stroke you are making. For service recognition, the Japanese employ a code (like this), a signal discreetly made under the table with the free hand informs the partner exactly what to expect. Hasegawa is the server in this case, and his mixed doubles partner is Miss Konno.*

PICTURE 124. *Karenza Matthews and Mary Wright (England) have devised their own signals code. From Karenza's one finger sign Mary knows in advance what type of service her partner intends to make.*

PICTURE 125. *A further example of the understanding between Hasegawa and Konno is the way they leave the table completely clear for each other's forehand shots.*

PICTURES 126 and 127. *The Russian pair, Misses Grinberg and Rudnova (backs to camera) are standing so close together in play against the Choi sisters (Korean Republic) they seem in danger of impeding one another during stroke play.*

But as Picture 127 shows, Miss Grinberg has no sooner made her return than she moves back, right out of range, making ample room for the powerful, penhold-grip forehand of her partner.

PICTURES 128, 129. *A right- and left-handed combination, like that of Alan Hydes and Pauline Piddock (England), is ideal because it enables either partner to play forehand or backhand without the necessity of elaborate arrangements for keeping out of each other's way. In this case the strong forehands of the English pair quickly dominated the exchanges with Gomez and Noriyama, of Peru.*

PICTURES 130–132. *World doubles champions in both 1967 and 1969, Alser and Johansson (Sweden) have developed uncanny understanding.*
PICTURE 130. *Johansson is closely watching his partner's backhand topspin service so he can judge accurately what type of return to expect.*

PICTURE 131. *Here Alser stands centrally to receive forehand, while Johansson waits behind, and to his right. However, the Swedish pair's understanding is so good they can automatically change their system during play if necessary, from the in and out to the circling method.*

PICTURE 132. *Alser has quickly retreated to make room for Johansson who rushes in to make an emergency return.*

PICTURES 133–138. *Both the 'in and out' and 'circling' systems are well illustrated in this sequence of play by Gomoskov and Amelin (USSR), opposing Andersson and Neidert (Sweden).*
PICTURE 133. *Amelin prepares to take Neidert's service on his backhand, thus leaving plenty of room for his partner's forehand to follow.*

PICTURE 134. *Amelin's backhand shot packs a lot of power, and it paves the way for . . .*

Picture 135. *Gomoskov's angled forehand.*

Picture 136. *Andersson's return has forced Amelin to take the next shot on the backhand wing, but anticipating this Gomoskov has moved smartly back and is going round behind his partner.*

PICTURE 137. *Having moved round Amelin, Gomoskov plays a powerful, well-angled backhand, which Neidert is just able to return . . .*

PICTURE 138. *. . . only for Amelin to make* this *'kill' to win the point.*

PICTURES 139, 140. *A good illustration of the whirlwind hitting of the Japanese champions in doubles action. In this case Hasakawa, partnering Tasaka, makes both the 'kills' against the USA pair Tannehill and Cowan.*

PICTURES 141–142. *Stanek and Miko, the famous Czech pair, are seen in action against Ezz and Salama (United Arab Republic). The Czechs specialise in short jabs from backhand, as well as forehand, keeping their opponents continually on the move. These tactics give them just the returns they seek in order to unleash powerful forehands.*

Stanek is shown in play. His partner, Miko, is noted for the variety of sidespin pushes he uses to spread-eagle the opposition.

PICTURES 143–146. *Langan and Caffery (Ireland) form another successful left- and right-handed combination boasting a close understanding. The Irishmen are shown in action against Pederson and Lüthje of Denmark.*
PICTURE 143. *Jimmy Langan serving from the backhand so Tommy Caffery will have plenty of room to come in with his powerful forehand.*

PICTURE 144. *When Caffery makes a forehand serve, Langan stands wide, but is ready to step in at once when Caffery has completed his shot and started to retreat.*

PICTURES 145 and 146. *How the Irish forehands come into play, each partner leaving plenty of room for the other.*

Chapter Six **Tactics**

In table tennis, as in boxing or fencing, you are matching wits with an opponent at very close range. As the ball leaves his bat you must decide in a split-second the direction, speed and spin of his shot. Then you must instantly take up position, make the appropriate return, and prepare for the next shot.

To master different types of opponent many different techniques are necessary. And besides quick reflexes you need stamina, courage, pliability, plus a keen tactical brain.

It is in tactics that I see the biggest opportunity for advancing the standard of play in the 'seventies. With the introduction of the sandwich bat in the 1950s the game first went through a 'hit or miss' era, since when the attacking game has reached a fantastically high standard.

Life has become hard for the wholly defensive player. No one could wish to see a better, nor more consistent defensive artist than Ebby Scholer, of West Germany; yet in Europe, at least, he has failed to dominate as he might have done in an earlier era. Once familiar with Scholer's game, European opponents drive him back from the table with high loops and finally pierce his defence with their 'kill'. However, on the world scene Scholer has enjoyed considerable success against the Asian champions, largely because his defensive game is comparatively strange to them.

With eight out of ten top players favouring attack, the current pattern is one of hit and counter-hit, with victory belonging to the one who consistently hits fastest, hardest and most accurately.

But what do you do when you find, after playing a few points, your opponent is able to hit faster and harder than you can yourself? The majority make the natural, but suicidal mistake of trying to speed up their normal game and to hit harder than the other man. Nearly always the result is that they make so many unforced errors that they ultimately beat themselves.

When this has happened in an international match, my advice to the England player concerned has been as follows: 'Try going back one pace, then re-adjust your swing and timing to take the ball later. Stay longer with the ball during your stroke, and return it with as much depth as possible'.

It isn't easy to re-adjust your approach in the middle of a match, but more than once a player has followed my advice with satisfying results. Finding the sudden change of pace difficult to master, the opponent has automatically responded by speeding up his own game until it is he who starts making the unforced errors.

The point is that to win the battle of tactics you must control the rallies. Once you lose control, and allow your opponent to dictate, you are on a hiding to nothing. This applies as much today as ever it did.

When opposing a player known to be better, or more experienced than yourself, gaining initial control, or regaining control once lost, is difficult; but always possible if you are able to surprise him out of his normal rhythm.

Quite often, recently, I have seen a player break up the pattern of hit and counter-hit with a sudden, vicious chop stroke. This has scored not only by its unexpectedness, but because many players have got out of the habit of dealing with backspin. The chop, therefore, has temporarily become a potential means of offence, as well as defence.

Any shot that achieves successful results seems quickly to get overworked. The topspin loop is a good example. In the early 'sixties this stroke tied up nearly everyone in knots, and gained the reputation of being more puzzling than the Indian rope trick. It was even said that this was a stroke without any answer, but given time, and practice against it, we not only found the answer but reduced the loop to nothing more fearsome than a tactical variation.

In the first place, high loop topspin can only be used really effectively against backspin. So if you use topspin yourself, or alternatively a straightforward push, the loop drive cannot be used against you with any real menace.

The loop can be countered by taking the ball early, smothering the spin before it can have much effect; or late, delaying one's return until nearly all the spin has worn off. This is not difficult with practice, since by its nature the loop is a stroke which must be clearly telegraphed in advance by the actions of any player using it.

Looping the loop, or swapping one loop for another, has become quite common in top championship play. This involves highly advanced technique, though to the top-class player it is merely a matter of adjustment in timing.

It now seems unlikely that anyone can invent a completely new stroke, using standard modern equipment, or that the speed of play and hitting power can be much increased. So we are left with tactics as the only major field for improvement, but bearing in mind the enormous number of stroke combinations and variations already available, this is vast.

You may see a top match today in which only two main strokes are used by both players, one to make an opening, the other to make the 'kill'. All shots are aimed either short, or deep. Both players realise that any return of mid-table length would promptly be 'killed'. So in effect modern table tennis is played on less than half the table surface available. Surely this, too, suggests scope for future development.

All the signs are that in the next few years the all-round stroke player will come back into his own with a game of great subtlety and infinite variety.

It is by variation and surprise that one can upset an opponent's rhythm, causing him to misread your shots and mistime his own.

The Asians have already shown us a glimpse of the tremendous range of spin services it is possible to use. We know that while backspin is the natural counter to topspin, it is perfectly possible to employ topspin against topspin, or backspin against backspin by a simple adjustment of bat angle and timing.

We have always seen that forehand shots need not all be made from the forehand wing, but from any part of the court. Then again, a whole new range of 'dummy' shots are possible which make an opponent doubt the evidence of his own eyes.

Armed with such weapons, plus supreme physical fitness and

a keen tactical brain, the champion of the 'seventies will indeed be a *formidable* opponent.

Special Note

As a sound method of learning all the strokes, and how to combine them, I strongly recommend practice on the lines of the ETTA Proficiency Award Tests detailed in *Appendix 2*.

Chapter Seven **Captaincy**

All clubs have a playing, or non-playing captain, but good ones are difficult to find. This is partly because the importance of good table tennis captaincy is not fully appreciated. Most people seem to think it involves little more than sitting on the sidelines and making encouraging noises from time to time. Believe me, there's a lot more in it than that!

Good players don't necessarily make good captains. Yet I think it essential that the captain should be, or should once have been a good player in at least the class in which his team is involved. He must know exactly what his players are going through, whether the match be an ordinary league fixture or a world championship final before a 'live' audience of 10,000, and many thousands more watching on TV.

During a match you've got to live every point with your players, yet not get over-excited; they look to you for calmness and control. At the same time, you dare not give the appearance of being bored–and during a long tournament that can be more difficult to avoid than you realise.

Often your experience will tell you that one of your players is adopting mistaken tactics. But do you have the ability to put this fact over to him, and put him right in the few minutes available between games when you are permitted to advise him?

Sometimes you have to say: 'You aren't following through properly with your shots', or 'Stop trying to rush him, try retreating more', and you can tell by the way he receives your comments they are not getting through. He just doesn't believe you, because you have yet to win his full confidence.

No matter, you must say what you have to say. Your players must learn that you are fully involved, and care about them.

Next time, however, perhaps you'll phrase your comments in a different manner to this particular player. He may react better to discussion and suggestion, rather than to direct criticism.

But most players, I find, welcome advice and follow it gladly. Thanks to your intervention they know they have someone else sharing the responsibility, someone else to blame if things go wrong!

A good team manger will accept such blame; but never expect any credit when his ideas prove successful.

Coaching from the sidelines during play is officially frowned upon, but many team managers use signals, or whispered instruction when their player approaches the surrounds in order to retrieve the ball. Many a captain's tip like: 'Short service to his forehand' has been instrumental in the winning of a championship.

But while it is possible to help one player to make a decision when he is at a loss, similar advice to another might cause a fatal break in his concentration. You've got to know your players inside out, their current form, and also their personal problems, though most of these you will no doubt have attempted to solve before the start of the match.

In my view, the most important part of the captain's job is what he does before and after a match. First comes supervision of the match preparations, then the travelling arrangements to the match.

Obviously long-distance journeys on the day of the match itself should be avoided if possible. Ideally I like my team to arrive at a venue about lunchtime before an evening match, when I try to arrange for them to have at least two hours' practice under the actual match conditions.

Those conditions will not always be to your players' liking. The tables, or the lighting, may not be as good as they are used to, or they may consider the floor too slippery. If improvements are possible, you do your best to convince the organisers they must be made. Otherwise you must persuade your players to accept the conditions as they are. After all, the players who can overcome the difficulties best are the ones who will win.

After practice I see that my players perform half-an-hour's physical training, each limbering up by means of those exercises which suit him best; whenever practical we go outside in the fresh air for this session. A tea meal usually follows, then a period of relaxation. We aim to arrive at the hall at least half-an-hour before the scheduled start of play, to get used to the atmosphere but also to put in a warming-up practice session.

As captain it is my responsibility to check the smartness of the players' turnout, also to ensure that they know the drill and timing for any pre-match parade or introductions.

In some matches the order of play becomes a complicated matter, and also one of vital importance. It is the captain's job to know the rules, and to take full advantage of them. Often it is not necessary to declare one's order of play until five minutes from the start. In such cases I normally ask each of my leading players: 'Ideally, which opponent would you like to meet first?' I then try to juggle our order to satisfy them, and nine times out of ten each gets what he wants.

Individual tournament events can be still more complicated. Every international tournament has a Jury, and the conduct of the captain at Jury meetings can be vital to his team's chances. Not only must he know the rules backwards, but be prepared to argue them diplomatically against decisions which could handicap his own players.

For example, it may be that following the withdrawal of a certain player the Jury propose moving one of your players to his less advantageous position in the draw. Bearing in mind that your words will be translated into three or four different languages, and then given various interpretations, a protest like 'Over my dead body!' may not have quite the effect intended. How much better if you could say truthfully and tactfully: 'I would entirely agree with your decision if only the rules permitted, but unfortunately we must comply with rule so-and-so'. But to be able to confound any Jury in this manner, of course, you must first do your homework.

Then again, in an international tournament today all matches are scheduled for certain tables at the outset, so as captain one must take every possible opportunity of getting each player used to the table and surrounds where he is due to play his next important round. But then, because another match is over-running, a tournament organiser may decide at the last moment to allocate your player a table other than the one originally scheduled. Having conditioned himself to a certain atmosphere, your player's confidence might now be upset, so you at once consider what sort of case you might put up to get the original arrangement restored. Success, or otherwise, could depend on the sort of relationship you have built up over the years with the organiser concerned.

You may come to the conclusion that in this instance you have no case, so the change must be accepted. All your powers of persuasion must now be exercised on your player. You might tell him: 'What does it matter to you which table you're on? Yesterday they moved you to table 2 and you beat so-and-so. As a matter of fact I think you played better on table 2 than on the other. So, you see, this move could be to your advantage!'

Oh yes, kidology can get you anywhere–as any soccer manager will testify.

But there will be times when no amount of persuasion can mollify the player, so an appeal to the organiser becomes your only hope. Organisers can be difficult, too, but there have been times when I have managed to keep an argument going until the match on the occupied table has been completed, by which time the organiser has no longer had any good reason for denying me my wish.

When your players realise you are prepared to fight every obstacle on their behalf they may begin to respect you. This respect is vital. It makes all the difference when you need to be very strict and tough with them, which may be quite often in the interests of team discipline.

All captains must study the tactical side, and must also know exactly what their players are capable of doing. For example, it is no good telling one chap to go for a forehand kill when he can't hit forehand to save his life.

When time permits I encourage a player to study his next opponent, after which I call a team conference and invite each member to give his opinions about the tactics our player should adopt. From their own experience of opposing this particular opponent, team members will pick his game to pieces until when our man goes into action, he knows exactly who he is up against, and what he has to do to beat him. He also feels confident in the knowledge that the rest of the team are right behind him in all his efforts.

By the way, we consider it OK for the average player to

watch his team-mates in action until about five minutes before his own game is due to begin. At that stage I like him to go off behind the scenes, with our trainer if possible, for 5 minutes' limbering-up exercises. I usually find when the player returns, his mind is clear, and his manner composed.

If my player, or his opponent, decides to take the 5 minute break after the third game in a five game match, I like to take him to one side for a quiet discussion about how the match is going. It is important that his concentration should not be entirely broken.

A good idea, I find, is for the non-playing captain to log his players' matches. Consulting my notes made in the heat of battle has enabled me to analyse faults, often to convince a player of faults he didn't realise he had. For example, I might say: 'Do you realise that in your last game you lost ten points trying to score on the backhand? That shot of yours normally works well, but you must face the fact it isn't working in this match, so why not be content to place your backhand shots and try to get in with your forehand instead? Once you establish a good lead and feel better, you can start going for those backhands again'.

After every match, conducting the inquest and detailing practice to remedy faults are further important tasks for the captain. In this respect I myself have been greatly helped by the fact that most important international matches and tournaments are now televised, and both BBC and ITV have been most co-operative in allowing my players to see replays of the films which are most enlightening. Imagine the benefit of being able to tell one's players: 'Don't just take my word for it–see for yourself how it was'.

Chapter Eight **Training, Fitness and Practice**

The champions of the 1970s are fitter than most of their predecessors, but if further improvement is to be made they must become fitter still. Training must be thoroughly professional, and really gruelling.

Poor footwork remains a common fault among young players in Britain. It lags stubbornly behind other departments. This can derive from slow anticipation. If a player is anticipating well, he has more time to move into good positions. But more often it is due to lack of training, fitness and practice.

Regular sprinting over short distances helps to develop quickness off the mark, while skipping is first-class for improving footwork and agility. No one has any excuse for not doing such exercises. At least you can sprint for your bus or train every day, or up and down stairs and escalators; and also carry out ten minutes' skipping-rope work in the garden. When skipping, it is a good idea to bring in the footwork used for the various strokes.

Practise 'shadowing' strokes, on an imaginary table against an imaginary opponent, as the Chinese champions do; or during a practice session at the table, try taking the ball sideways on one wing only; you'll find you have to move very quickly indeed to play shots in this manner. Never allow yourself to be caught flat-footed. Always stand on the balls of the feet.

During a game you shouldn't have to think about your feet. All movements should be instinctive. But remember, the only way of playing faster, and hitting harder, is to get into position for each shot sooner.

For stamina and general fitness I used to do pre-season training with the professional footballers of Spurs and Crystal Palace. Modern stars follow a similar routine; Denis Neale, for example, trains with Middlesbrough FC. But if you lack such special facilities, there is nothing to stop you from working out your own programme of sprinting, skipping, deep breathing exercises and roadwork.

Build up gradually. Roadwork should be split into periods of steady jogging, walking, and short sprints, starting with 2 miles and working up to about 5. This becomes less of a grind when done with friends.

However, these days most clubs have devised highly scientific training programmes of their own, with Special Circuit Training exercises, progress being checked against the clock. In this connection, I am indebted to the England trainer-coach *Les Gresswell* for the expert advice which follows to the end of this chapter.

Three main practices will help the advanced players to improve (1) Physical training (2) Pressure table tennis (3) Table tennis practices in general.

Physical Training

Advanced players have one thing in common: they are playing to win and to win when it really counts. To do this they must prepare themselves for certain peaks during a season. This is possible through *seasonal* training, performed at intervals when it will provide maximum benefit.

Bear in mind what fitness qualities every top-class player seeks:

1. Mobility and flexibility
2. Speed of movement (sharp reactions)
3. Muscular co-ordination and strength
4. Stamina (general endurance).

The English playing season lasts from September to April. The main aim 'out of season' is to build up strength and stamina. Let's analyse this:

MAY–Aim: to stop all table tennis play and concentrate on the four main fitness qualities. Stamina training should include long-distance running (up to 5 miles) and short-sprints. Muscular strengthening is performed through circuits, concentrating on the upper girdle region.

JUNE–Aim: again no table tennis play, but even harder physical work. In addition to long runs, introduce 'shuttle runs' which are frequent short sprints performed against a target-time. Strength work should be aimed at upper body regions. Circuit–twice per week.
JULY–Similar to June, but to include pressure training on the table tennis table. Strengthening work should now be concentrated on the legs. Any form of 'overload' on the legs is satisfactory–circuits, double-jumps, and other games activities.
AUGUST–More pressure training on the table. Gradual tailing off of physical work. Stamina once per week, and leg circuit also once.
SEPT–APRIL–Under 'in season' conditions the two main qualities are Mobility (gaining suppleness) and Speed training. How much you do depends on the amount of table tennis competition in which you are involved. The general pattern should be to carry out maximum training initially, but gradually to tail-off as the date of the competitive event gets nearer.

Mobility

Try to keep supple by exercising each and every day, and *always* before a table tennis practice session. The main aims of mobility training are:

1. to keep ligaments and joints loose
2. to help joints respond to muscular movements
3. to stimulate the body and nervous system
4. to help those twisting, bending and swinging movements, indispensable in every match.

The following exercises can be performed daily, and are particularly important before table tennis practice sessions. They are given in order:

1. *Arm Movements* Flexing and shaking wrists, fingers and elbows. Arm swings, forward and backward rotation.
2. *Shoulder and Head* Touching shoulder blades together, rotating shoulders forward and backward.
   Neck Exercises Rock head either way, also up and down.

3. *Trunk Exercises* (Attacking the spinal region.)
   Touching alternate toes with hands.
   Rotating spine (many exercises suitable, including thigh stretch).
4. *Leg Exercises* To include straddle hops, splits, leg kicks, knee and ankle rotation.

Points to emphasise in the many different exercises used for Mobility Training are:

1. They must be done every day for about 10 minutes.
2. Maximum effort (that is complete contraction) is essential.
3. They can be performed either at home, or in a table tennis hall.

Speed Conditioning

This is very specialised work, so the tasks should be supervised by a qualified trainer. However, there are certain combinations common to all, which advanced players could use without supervision.

The aims are:

1. to increase control, and delivery in table tennis movements
2. to sharpen reactions and co-ordination
3. to speed up mental capacity
4. to increase anticipation.

The player can choose any of his own movements and practice them in combinations:

1. *Shadow Practice* Build up certain strokes, such as a combination of forehand and backhand drives, stringing them together. Perform 3 times at 30 seconds, with 30 seconds' rest interval between each attempt. This practice can usefully be performed in front of a large mirror.
2. *Exaggerated Movement* Perform given strokes with over-deliberation on certain points. For example, follow through after a hit with full knees bend, knees to touch floor. Chase wide returns: or perform a loop drive, with full body action. This helps develop speed.

3. *Side Shuttles* As in sideways table tennis movements. (a) Putting alternate knees on the ground from the 'ready' position. (b) Side Jumps. Jumping sideways, using leg as an axis, and landing in low, crouched position.
4. Performing given tasks to a *set number pattern*, say 1 to 4. Partner shouts any number between 1 and 4. The player must respond with the appropriate movement, agreed beforehand. This helps to sharpen reactions.

I've been able to give merely a general outline of the amount of training necessary. It requires special study. For maximum benefit to be gained, bear in mind the following important considerations in training:

1. Relaxation.
2. Diet (correct nutrition is essential to maintain good condition).
3. Sleep, regular habits, and a stable existence.
4. The realisation that both smoking and excessive drinking of alcohol, are dangerous practices for the athlete.
5. A general understanding of what is required.

Pressure Training on the Table (for two or more players)

The programme should start under the coach's supervision with simple limbering-up to loosen neck, wrists, arms, shoulders, trunk, knees and ankles. Next come the basic movements used in play, such as turning to backhand and forehand from the basic 'ready' position; moving to the left and right when facing the table; moving in, and out, on the forehand and backhand lines. Next, essential movements are combined, such as the left-right movement with the in-out.

Practice on the table begins with an all round warm-up session for all the players involved, using several balls. Next comes attention to individual stroke production. For example, the coach may make a series of varied services to all points of the table, inviting each player in turn to practice such returns as the half-volley, slow push, or chop.

Pressure is gradually increased, the player being required to alternate forehand with backhand, or to switch forehand drives and forehand pushes while the coach makes chop and push returns on the same line.

After practising stroke combinations on one line of play, we introduce combinations which involve turning, like the short backhand push alternated with the long forehand chop. All balls must be returned to a specified target area, while the coach alternates a drop shot to one target with a topspin drive to another. All the time pressure is gradually increased.

Here are some advanced Pressure Tasks for a combination of two players with one ball:

1. *To develop sideways movement and forehand control* Player A is the feeder. From the centre of the table he deflects the ball alternately to backhand and forehand court. Player B is required to return all the balls to the middle of the table with forehand topspin drives. Time – 5 minutes.
2. *For service and follow-up practice* Player B serves from the backhand court. Player A blocks across court to the forehand. Player B chases the ball for a 'kill'. Time – 5 minutes.
3. *Killing practice* Player A and B play backhand-hit and counter-hit. Then, at a signal, player A switches his shot to B's forehand court. Player B must chase across and 'kill' the ball for an outright winner. Time – 5 minutes.

These three combinations can be varied, and many other systems are available to help players in actual match situations. Concentration and application are vital. And bear in mind, the feeder is just as important as the player under stress.

Table Tennis Practices

Competitive table tennis is now of such a high standard that it is no longer sufficient just to play practice games plus 'a few shots'. England's international squad, for example, has a set pattern for practice. Practice never lasts more than 2½ hours, and always starts with physical training. But the table tennis exercises are devised to suit the 'stage of the season'.

The main principles of squad practice are as follows:

1. Quality is important, probably even more important than quantity.

2. It is important to warm-up through regular routines before going on to the table.
3. Practice is not only for technique. It is also for concentration, application and, above all, self-discipline.
4. Both the 'feeder' and the 'receiver' gain benefits.
5. The only worthwhile practice is that conducted really seriously.
6. To help yourself, you must help others.

PICTURE 147. *Members of the England International squad pictured during a training session.*

PICTURE 148. *Jill Shirley pictured during Pressure Training for the England team. Her task here was to return service, run back to touch the wall with her bat, then return to the table in time to deal with the next service (timed by the 'feeder' to ensure maximum effort from Jill).*

Chapter Nine **Umpiring**

Every player should know how to umpire a match competently, not only because he will be expected to 'help out' with the umpiring in some of the tournaments in which he is a competitor, but because a study of the umpire's job is the best way of getting a good knowledge of the laws and how they should be interpreted.

You may find that you have a flair for this vital job, which would enable you to continue to play your part in the game long after your top class playing days have ended. To become an expert umpire demands just as much dedication as is needed to become an expert player, so those who qualify by examination to become County Umpires, and subsequently National Umpires (qualified to officiate at World Championships) can wear their badges with pride.

The umpire is an official to respect because in every match for which he is appointed, his decision is final. The only exception to this is when a line judge and stroke counter have also been appointed, when final decisions *within their province* belong to them. The line judge decides whether a ball striking the edge of the table is fairly 'on' or 'off', also by special arrangement certain other tricky questions; while the stroke counter is only concerned after the 'expedite system' (Law 16) has been put into effect.

Neither individual players, nor team captains can modify a decision on fact by the umpire, line judge or stroke counter. Only for a decision on conduct not covered by the laws may an appeal be made to the referee.

The umpire has the dual responsibility of seeing that the match is conducted fairly, also in a manner that spectators can follow as easily as possible. His standards of dress and conduct must always be beyond reproach.

To carry out his duties, the best position for him to take up is between 2 and 3 m from the side of the table in line with the net. If a raised chair has not been provided, he will find it better to stand for doubles to ensure a clear view of the centre line.

Players are normally entitled to a knock-up of not more than two minutes before a match. The right of choice of ends or service is decided by tossing a coin. The umpire should note the name of the player due to serve first, and in doubles that of the first receiver. Once the order of play has been established in the first game of a doubles match, the order in all subsequent games is automatic.

The umpire must satisfy himself that all equipment and dress, the height of the net, and other regulations are in order. He should also test that his microphone and amplifying equipment, if provided, are working satisfactorily.

The names of the contestants, the event and round in which they are competing and the number of games to be played should be announced before the start of the match. If necessary, players should be separately identified for the spectators' benefit. Immediately before play begins in each game the player due to serve first should be named, and the score 'love-all' announced.

The score in games should be announced after each game.

Accurate, clear and correctly timed calling of the score is a most important part of the umpire's duties. The score should be called immediately the ball is out of play, giving first the server's score, then that of the receiver. When a service change is due, the umpire reverses the score order, then adds the name of the new server.

The full number of points scored should be called throughout the game–for example, 4–4 or 4-all, also 20–20 or 20-all (but not 'deuce'). When first the score 10 is reached in the last possible game of a match, the umpire should call the score followed by the words: 'change ends, please' as soon as the rally finishes.

Otherwise he should not need to speak between rallies except to call the score, or to precede the score call with one of the following explanations:

Good service not made–'Fault'
Net touched by player, clothing or racket–'Touched net'

Playing surface moved–'Moved table'
Free hand touched playing surface – 'Hand on table'
Ball in contact with player over table – 'Over table'
Ball volleyed – 'Volley'
Ball bounced twice in same court – 'Not up'
Ball struck twice by one player – 'Double hit'
Ball struck by wrong player in doubles – 'Wrong player'

If he wishes to interrupt play for any reason the umpire should call 'Let'.

At the end of the match he should announce the result.

Apart from the need to make split-second decisions correctly an umpire is also expected to use tact and discretion in dealing with situations not precisely covered by the laws. A good umpire understands the pressure under which players are competing, and makes allowances for very minor, or marginal infringements.

However, it is vitally important never to show weakness or indecision, so destroying the player's faith, prejudicing a fair result, and spoiling the spectators' enjoyment.

Appendix One THE LAWS OF TABLE TENNIS

(As adopted by the International Table Tennis Federation)

Note: These rules have been reproduced, almost word for word, from section 6 of the ITTF's official book of regulations and recommendations. For the purposes of this book, therefore, disregard the first digit (6) in the cross-references: to cross-refer to, for example, the reference '6.17.1.1.' in 1.4 below, simply turn to rule 17.1.1.

SINGLES

1. THE TABLE

1.1. The table shall be in surface rectangular, 274 cm (9 ft) in length, 152·5 cm (5 ft) in width; it shall be supported in such a way that its upper surface shall be 76 cm (2 ft 6 in) above the floor, and shall lie in a horizontal plane.

1.2. It shall be made of any material and shall yield a uniform bounce of not less than 22 cm (8¾ in) and not more than 25 cm (9¾ in) when a standard ball, preferably of medium bounce, is dropped from a height of 30·5 cm (12 in) above its surface.

1.3. The upper surface of the table shall be termed the 'playing surface'; it shall be matt, colour very dark, preferably dark green, with a white line 2 cm (¾ in) broad along each edge.

1.4. The lines at the 152·5 cm edges or ends of the playing surface shall be termed 'end lines'. The lines at the 274 cm edges or sides of the playing surface shall be termed 'side lines'. (Note: For Doubles Centre Line on Singles table surface see 6.17.1.1.)

1.5. *Recommendations*

1.5.1. The table surface shall be of hard wood and either sprayed (for preference) or painted, but not freshly painted–for fresh colour is apt to come off on the ball surface–with a dull green cellulose lacquer or paint.

1.5.2. The table must be rigidly constructed.

1.5.3. If any lettering appear on the ends it should not be white; off-white would be suitable.

1.6. *Specification: Matt Surface* (Applicable also to 6.3 and 6.4.)

1.6.1. The glossiness of a surface measured with an EEL Glossometer (45° gloss head setting) should in no case exceed 6 and should preferably not exceed 2. Corresponding measurements with an ASTM/60° standard or Gardner instrument at 60° angle should in no case exceed 24 and should preferably not exceed 6. (Standard of reflection: polished black gloss equals 100.) In any case glossiness that enables the shapes of light sources to be distinguished should be regarded as excessive, and eliminated as soon as possible.

1.6.2. The requirement of a 'matt' surface for the Table (6.1), the Ball (6.3), and the Racket (6.4), is to prevent a dazzling reflection of light from distracting the eye of the player. As well as discouraging the use of shiny materials in actual play. Associations should take positive steps, by an approach to manufacturers, importers and dealers and by approving the use only of matt materials, to ensure that satisfactory equipment, complying with this specification, is available.
(Note: For positioning of table in tournament hall playing space, see 6.26.2.)

2. THE NET AND ITS SUPPORTS

2.1. The playing surface shall be divided into two courts of equal size by a net running parallel to the end lines and 137 cm (4 ft 6 ins) from each. The net, with its suspension, shall be 183 cm (6 ft) in length; its upper part along its whole length shall be 15·25 cm (6 ins) above the playing surface; its lower part along the whole length shall be close to the playing surface. The net shall be suspended by a cord attached at each end to an upright post 15·25 cm (6 ins) high; the outside limits of each post shall be 15·25 cm (6 ins) outside the side line.

2.2. *Recommendations*

2.2.1. The net should be of a dark shade of green, and should be of an unsized (soft) mesh not less than 7·5 mm nor more than 12·5 mm square. It should have a white top, depending from the cord suspension, not more than 15mm wide. (Note that in accordance with Law 2.1, which provides that the net shall be suspended by a cord, only one cord–a single horizontal cord–may suspend the net and the attachment of the net to the post, if any, must be so loose as not to exert tension and thereby constitute a suspension.)

2.2.2. The diameter of the post should not exceed 22 mm and any device for adjusting the height or tension of the cord suspending the net should be situated at the base of the post, should not project more than 7 mm from the post.

3. THE BALL

3.1. The ball shall be spherical. It shall be made of celluloid or a similar plastic, white and matt; it shall not be less than 37·2 mm (1·46 ins) nor more than 38·2 mm (1·50 ins) in diameter; it shall not be less than 2·40 gm (37 grains) nor more than 2·53 gm (39 grains) in weight.

3.2. *Specification: Bounce*

The standard bounce required shall be not less than 235 mm (9¼ ins) and not more than 255 mm (10 ins) when the ball is dropped from a height of 305 mm (12 ins) on a specially designed steel block. Balls rebounding 235–241 mm are described as low-bounce, 242–248 mm as medium-bounce and 249–255 mm as high-bounce.

3.3. Only a brand of ball approved for the purpose as provided below (6.3.2 and 4) may be used in World Championships, in Open International Table Tennis Competitions, or in International Matches unless otherwise agreed by the participating Associations.

3.3.1. Samples of brands of ball to be approved may be submitted for test only by the Association in whose territory the wholesale firm issuing the given brand of ball is situated. No correspondence may be entered into direct with firms. Samples should be addressed to the Equipment Committee, with a copy of the application for test to the Hon General Secretary of the Federation. Application for test must be accompanied by a fee to cover expenses, to be determined by the Advisory Committee, which may also decide a further appropriate fee if approval is given. A report of the examination shall be returned to the submitting Association and, with recommendation, to the Advisory Committee.

3.3.2. The Advisory Committee may grant approval for choice by the respective organising Associations for use in World Championships, Open International Competitions and International Matches, or it may withhold approval. Decisions shall be notified to all member Associations.

3.3.3. Where approval is given the issuing firm may advertise the brand approved as 'Approved by ITTF', but only provided such advertisement is always accompanied by the date. When a ball is approved between July and December, approval shall be dated the current season and the succeeding season; when it is approved between January and June, it shall be dated the two succeeding seasons.

3.3.4. Dates for submission of samples shall be fixed by the Equipment Committee but further samples of a brand once examined may not be submitted for examination until at least twelve months have elapsed from the date of decision on the previous submission.

3.3.5. *Note:* Approval certifies only that the submitted samples of the brand approved have been found to conform to the specifications in the laws with a high degree of regularity. Balls tend to vary in mass production and Associations are recommended to make their own arrangements with the wholesaler concerned to ensure the availability of supplies approaching the standard certified as attained by the samples of any given brand.

4. THE RACKET

4.1. The racket may be of any size, shape or weight. Its surface shall be dark coloured and matt. The blade shall be of wood, continuous, of even thickness, flat and rigid. If the blade is covered on either side, this covering may be either–

4.1.1. of plain, ordinary pimpled rubber, with pimples outward, of a total thickness of not more than 2 mm; or–

4.1.2. of 'sandwich', consisting of a layer of cellular rubber surfaced by plain ordinary pimpled rubber–turned outwards or inwards–in which case the total thickness of covering of either side shall not be more than 4 mm.

4.2. When rubber is used on both sides of a racket, the colour shall be similar; when wood is used for either side or for both sides, it should be dark, either naturally, or by being stained (not painted) in such a way as not to change the friction-character of its surface.

4.3. *Note:* The part of the blade nearest the handle and gripped by the fingers may be covered with cork or other materials for convenience of grip; it is to be regarded as part of the handle.

4.4. *Note:* If the reverse side of the racket is never used for striking the ball, it may all be of cork or any other material convenient for gripping. The limitation of racket cover materials refers only to the striking surface. A stroke with a side covered with cork or any other gripping surface would, however, be illegal and result in a lost point.

4.5. *Specification: Pimpled Rubber*
A single covering with pimples evenly distributed not fewer than 10 nor more than 50 to the square centimetre (65–325 to the square inch) on rubber which, whether natural or synthetic, is non-cellular, and of which the total thickness includes the height of the pimples and adhesive.

4.6. *Specification: Dark Colour* (Applicable also to *Clothes* 6.24.)

4.6.1. Colours that give a 'Y' value under illuminant A of less than 30 per cent according to the CIE system may be considered sufficiently dark, either for clothing or rackets. A colour card is available for guidance.

4.6.2. As well as discouraging the wearing of light materials or use of light coloured racket surfaces in actual play, Associations should take positive steps, by an approach to manufacturers, and dealers, and by approving dark materials, to ensure that uniform or otherwise suitable types of wear, and racket surfaces that comply with the specification, are available.

5. THE ORDER OF PLAY: DEFINITIONS

5.1. The player who first strikes the ball during a rally shall be termed the server.

5.2. The player who next strikes the ball during a rally shall be termed the receiver.

5.3. The server shall first make a good service, the receiver shall then make a good return, and thereafter server and receiver shall each alternately make a good return.

5.4. The period during which the ball is in play shall be termed a rally.

5.5. A rally the result of which is not scored shall be termed a let.

5.6. A rally the result of which is scored shall be termed a point.

6. A GOOD SERVICE

6.1. The ball shall be placed on the palm of the free hand, which must be stationary, and above the level of the playing surface. Service shall commence by the server projecting the ball by hand only, without imparting spin, near vertically upwards, so that the ball is visible at all times to the Umpire, and so that it visibly leaves the palm. As the ball is then descending from the height of its trajectory, it shall be struck so that it touches the server's court and then, passing directly over or around the net, touches the receiver's court.

6.1.1. *Note:* Missed Service: Note that, if a player, in attempting to serve, miss the ball altogether, it is a lost point because the ball was in play from the moment it left his hand and a good service has not been made of the ball already in play.
Definitions for above (6.1)–

6.1.2. 'Struck':

'Struck' means 'hit with the racket or with the racket hand' which, for this purpose, shall be understood as included in the racket. The racket hand is the hand carrying the racket; the free open hand is the hand not carrying the racket. Therefore, a return effected with the hand alone, after dropping the racket, is 'not good' for it is no longer the 'racket hand'; a return effected by the racket alone, after it has slipped or been thrown from the hand, is likewise 'not good', for the ball is not 'struck'. (See also 6.4.4.)

6.1.3. 'Touching the court' (Edge Balls):

6.1.3.1. The phrase Table Surface (comprising the courts) is to be interpreted as including the top edges of the table-top, and a ball in play which strikes these latter is therefore good and still in play; though if it strikes the side of the table-top below the edge, it becomes dead and counts against the last striker.

6.1.3.2. The direction in which the ball is travelling since it was last struck, its spin, and the direction in which it rebounds from the edge can all help to distinguish between a 'good' ball that has touched the edge and a 'bad' ball that has made contact below the edge. If the point of contact of the ball has occurred at the end or side of the table away from the striker it must nearly always have been a 'good' touch; only an exceptionally heavy spin could have brought about a contact completely below the edge. If the contact has occurred on the same side of the table as that from which the ball was struck, it may, however, have occurred below the edge and if the rebound in this case is directly downward this is a sign that the contact must have been 'bad', i.e. against the side, below the edge.

6.1.4. 'Over or around the net'

If the ball, in passing over the net, or around the net, touches it or its supports, it shall, nevertheless, be considered to have passed directly, except for the purpose of Law 6.9.1. 'Around the net' shall be considered as being under or around the projection of the net and supports outside the side line. The net end should be close enough to the post to prevent the ball from passing between net and post and to pass so would not constitute 'around the net'.

6.2. The free hand, while in contact with the ball in service, shall be open, with the fingers together, thumb free and the ball resting on the palm without being cupped or pinched in any way by the fingers.

6.2.1. *Warning*

It is the responsibility of the server to serve so that the correctness of his service can be checked by the umpire. If the server is serving so that the umpire's view is obstructed, the umpire shall warn him and, on any subsequent occasion on which his view is obstructed, and he may have doubt about the correctness of the service, the umpire shall call a fault.

6.2.2. *Exception*

Strict observance of the prescribed method of service may be waived where the umpire is notified, before play begins, that compliance by the player in question is prevented by physical disability.

6.3. At the moment of the impact of the racket on the ball in service, the ball shall be behind the end line of the server's court or an imaginary extension thereof.

7. A GOOD RETURN

A ball having been served or returned in play shall be struck so that it pass directly over or around the net and touch directly the opponent's court, provided that, if the ball, having been served or returned in play, return with its own impetus over or around the net, it may be struck, while still in play, so that it touch directly the opponent's court.

8. IN PLAY

The ball is in play from the moment at which it is projected from the hand in service until:

8.1. It has touched one court twice consecutively.

8.2. It has, except in service, touched each court alternately without having been struck by the racket intermediately.

8.3. It has been struck by any player more than once consecutively or by any player out of proper sequence as provided by law 6.22.

8.4. It has touched any player or anything that he wears or carries, except his racket or his racket hand below the wrist.

8.5. On the volley it comes in contact with the racket or the racket hand below the wrist.

8.6. It has touched any object other than the net, supports, or those referred to above.

9. A LET
The rally is a let:

9.1. If the ball served in passing over the net touch it or its supports, provided the service either be otherwise good or be volleyed by the receiver.

9.1.1. *Definition: The Volley*
If the ball in play come into contact with the racket or racket hand, not yet having touched the playing surface on one side of the net since last being struck on the other side, it shall be said to have been volleyed.

9.2. If a service be delivered when the receiver or his partner is not ready, provided always that they may not be deemed to be unready if the receiver attempt to strike at the ball.

9.3. If any player be prevented by an accident, not under his control, from serving a good service or making a good return.

9.4. If either pair lose the point owing to an accident not within their control.

Notes to 6.9.3. and 6.9.4.

9.4.1. *Ball Fractured in Play*
If the ball split or become otherwise fractured in play,

affecting a player's return, the rally is a let. It is the umpire's duty to stop play, recording a let, when he has reason to believe that the ball in play is fractured or imperfect; and to decide those cases in which the faulty ball is clearly fractured in actually going out of play, and in no way handicaps the player's return, when the point should be scored. In all cases of doubt, however, he should declare a let.

9.4.2. *Fixtures*

A moving spectator, a neighbouring player, a sudden noise, i.e. any neighbouring object in movement (except a partner) should be regarded as an accident not under control, interference from which implies a let. A stationary spectator, fixed seating, the umpire, the light, a nearby table, a continuous sound of even volume, i.e. any relatively constant or motionless hazard, should not be so regarded, any complaint against interference from it during play should be regarded as void.

9.5. If it be interrupted as provided in Law 6.15 or Law 6.22.

10. A POINT

10.1. Except as provided in Law 6.9., either pair shall lose a point:

10.1.1. If the server fail to make a good service.

10.1.2. If a good service or a good return having been made by one of their opponents in proper sequence, they fail to make a good return.

10.1.3. If either partner, or his racket, or anything that he wears or carries touch the net or its supports while the ball is in play.

10.1.4. If either partner or his racket, or anything that he wears or carries, move the playing surface while the ball is in play.

10.1.5. If the free hand of either partner touch the playing surface while the ball is in play.

10.1.6. If, before the ball in play shall have passed over the end lines or side lines not yet having touched the playing surface on their side of the table since being struck by one of their opponents in proper sequence it come in contact with either partner or with anything that he wears or carries.

10.1.7. If at any time either partner volley the ball (see Definition 6.9.1.1.).

10.2. *Expedite System*

If a game (see 6.11 below) be unfinished fifteen minutes after it has begun, the rest of that game and the remaining games of the match shall proceed under the Expedite System. Thereafter, if the service and twelve following strokes of the server are returned by good returns of the receiver, the server shall lose the point.

11. A GAME

A game shall be won by the player who first wins 21 points, unless both players shall have scored 20 points, when the winner of the game shall be he who first wins two points more than his opponent.

12. A MATCH

12.1. A match shall consist of one game or the best of three or best of five games.

12.2. Play shall be continuous throughout, except that either opposing pair is entitled to claim a repose period of not more than five minutes' duration between the third and fourth games of a five-game match.

12.3. *Note:* This rule defines a contest between two players or pairs. A contest consisting of a group of individual matches between two sides is usually distinguished as a 'team match'.

13. THE CHOICE OF ENDS AND SERVICE

The choice of ends and the right to be servers or receivers in every match shall be decided by toss, provided that, if the winners of the toss choose the right to be servers or receivers, the other pair shall have the choice of ends, and vice-versa, and provided that the winners of the toss may, if they prefer it, require the other pair to make the first choice.

14. THE CHANGE OF ENDS AND SERVICE

14.1. *Ends*

The pair who started at one end in a game shall start at the other in the immediately subsequent game, and so on, until the end of the match. In the last possible game of the match, the pairs shall change ends when first either pair reaches the score 10.

14.2. *Service*

The pair who served first in a game shall be receivers first in the immediately subsequent game, and so on until the end of a match.

15. OUT OF ORDER OF ENDS OR SERVICE

15.1. *Ends*

If the players have not changed ends when ends should have been changed, the players shall change ends as soon as the mistake is discovered, unless a game has been completed since the error, when the error shall be ignored. In any circumstances, all points scored before the discovery shall be reckoned.

15.2. *Service*

If a player serve out of his turn, play shall be interrupted as soon as the mistake is discovered and shall continue with that player serving who, according to the sequence established at the beginning of the match, or at the score 10 if that sequence has been changed under Law 21, should be the server at the score that has been reached. In any circumstances, all points scored before the discovery shall be reckoned.

DOUBLES

16. The above Laws shall apply in the Doubles Game except as below.

17. THE TABLE

17.1. The surface of the table shall be divided into two parts by a white line 3 mm ($\frac{1}{8}$ in) broad, running parallel with the side lines and distant equally from each of them. This line shall be termed the centre line.

17.1.1. *Note:* The doubles centre line may be permanently marked in full length on the table. This is a convenience and in no way invalidates the table for singles play.

17.2. The part of the table surface on the nearer side of the net and the right of the centre line in respect to the server shall be called the server's right half-court, that on the left in respect to him the server's left half-court. The part of the table surface on the farther side of the net and the left of the centre line in respect to the server shall be called the receiver's right half-court, that on the right in respect to the server the receiver's left half-court.

18. A GOOD SERVICE

The service shall be delivered as otherwise provided in Law 6.6, and so that it touch first the server's right half-court or the centre line on his side of the net, and then passing directly over or around the net, touch the receiver's right half-court or the centre line on his side of the net.

19. THE ORDER OF PLAY

The server shall first make a good service, the receiver shall then make a good return, the partner of the server shall then make a good return, the partner of the receiver shall then make a good return, the server shall then make a good return and thereafter each player alternately in that sequence shall make a good return.

20. THE CHOICE OF THE ORDER OF PLAY

The pair who have the right to serve the first five services in any game shall decide which partner shall do so. In the first game of a match the opposing pair shall then decide similarly which shall be the first receiver. In subsequent games the serving pair shall choose their first server and the first receiver will then be established automatically to correspond with the first server as provided in 6.21.3 below.

21. THE ORDER OF SERVICE

21.1. Throughout each game, except as provided in the second paragraph, the first five services shall be delivered by the selected partner of the pair who have the right to do so and shall be received by the appropriate partner of the opposing pair. The second five services shall be delivered by the receiver of the first five services and received by the partner of the server of the first five services. The third five services shall be delivered by the partner of the server of the first five services and received by the partner of the receiver of the first five services. The fourth five services shall be delivered by the partner of the receiver of the first five services and received by the server of the first five services. The fifth five services shall be delivered as the first five services. And so on, in sequence, until the end of the game or the score 20-all or the introduction of the Expedite System, when the sequence of serving and receiving shall be uninterrupted, but each player shall serve only one service in turn until the end of the game.

21.2. In the last possible game of a match when first either player reaches the score 10 the receiving pair must alter its order of serving.

21.3. In each game of a match the initial order of receiving shall be opposite to that in the preceding game.

22. OUT OF ORDER OF RECEIVING

If a player act as receiver out of his turn play shall be interrupted as soon as the mistake is discovered and shall continue with that player receiving who, according to the sequence established at the beginning of the game or at the score 10 if that sequence has been changed under Law 6.21, should be receiver at the score which has been reached. In any circumstances all points scored before the discovering shall be reckoned.

23. FURTHER AMENDMENTS AND ADDITIONS

As applicable.

24. CLOTHING

24.1. Players shall not wear white or light coloured clothing which might tend to distract or unsight the opponent. Any badge or lettering on a playing garment must not be so large or conspicuous as to break disturbingly its uniform dark colour. The decision as to the offence under this rule shall be with the referee. (For Dark Colour Specification, see 6.4.6.)

24.2. Associations are recommended strongly to discourage practice before the public in non-playing dress or footwear.

25. FLOORING. RECOMMENDATION

Flooring should be not of stone or linoleum, but of hard, non-slippery rigid wood, not white or brightly reflecting. Caution should be observed in accepting composition flooring, for though this may give a fast game it is generally harder on the feet than wood.

26. PLAYING SPACE

26.1. At World Championships, Open International Championships, and International Matches where not otherwise agreed, the minimum playing space for each table shall be 14 metres (46 feet) long, 7 metres (23 feet) wide, and 4 metres (13 feet, 2 inches) high. It is recommended that at all other events the playing space should, if less, be as near this minimum as practicable and in any case not less than 12 metres (39 feet) by 6 metres (19½ feet).

26.2. Where there is more than one table these should be set side by side and not, where this is avoidable, one behind the other.

27. SURROUNDS. RECOMMENDATION

Dark surrounds about 75 cm (2 ft 6 ins) high should delimit the playing space, separating each match from any other match and from the public. The surrounds should be stable, but light enough to fall without injury to a player who may run into them.

28. BACKGROUND. RECOMMENDATION

The background should for preference be of a uniform dark green or another uniform dark colour, not light (or patchy) as this tends to unsight the players. Where there are spectators in the background, it is preferable for the light there to be subdued compared with that over the playing area and in no circumstances should naked lights at eye level or back-lighting by daylight through windows be present in the background.

29. LIGHTING

29.1. Measured at table height, the light shall be at least 400 lux in strength uniformly over the table, and not less than half the table strength over any other part of the playing area.

29.2. The light source shall be not less than 4 metres from the ground.

29.3. While general lighting alone is permissible if it gives this prescribed strength, wherever practicable a system providing special lighting over the table and playing area, and a contrasting relative darkness or less light outside the playing area is preferable in the interests of both players and spectators. (Note: See 6.28.)

29.4. It is preferable to avoid mixed daylight and artificial light.

29.5. Fluorescent lighting may cause difficulties where it is not three-phase.

 BRONZE AWARD TESTS

(a) SHORT-TOUCH SERVICES:
- (i) Serve 5 Short Forehand Services, i.e. to land short of a line marked 18″ from the net.
- (ii) As (i), but service with Backhand.
  Errors allowed: 3 (for 10 successes).

(b) LONG TOPSPIN SERVICES:
- (i) Serve 5 long Forehand Topspin Services, i.e. to land within 18″ of the distant baseline.
- (ii) As (i) but service with Backhand.
  Errors allowed: 3 (for 10 successes).

(c) ALL-FOREHAND PUSH-CONTROL:
(From 2 points, returned to 1 target.) Using sound footwork for training, return 40 Slow Push Shots, (which have been placed, slowly, by Controller, from 'A', alternately to Area 'C' and Area 'D'). Candidate to use only FOREHAND PUSH-STROKES, all played back to Area 'A'. (See diagram for Areas).
Errors allowed: 5.

(d) ALL-BACKHAND PUSH-CONTROL:
(From 2 points, returned to 1 target.) As (c) but Candidate to use only BACKHAND PUSH-STROKES, and to return all balls to Controller's Area 'B'.
Errors allowed: 5.

(e) FOREHAND AND BACKHAND PUSH-CONTROL (alternated):
Return 40 Slow pushes by playing BACKHAND PUSH

AND FOREHAND PUSH STROKES, strictly alternately and with due attention to correct execution, all balls to be kept within a channel 18″ wide. Controller places every ball to the same point.

Errors allowed: 5.

NOTES:

(i) For 'Penholder' Styles, for 'BACKHAND' read: 'To Left of the Body'.

(ii) For lefthanders, reverse targets ('A' for 'B', etc).

(iii) Two players may be tested simultaneously on one table by using opposite diagonal 'channels' on tests (a), (b), and (e).

SILVER AWARD TESTS

Preliminary: Candidate must have passed the 'Bronze' Tests.

(a) RETURN OF SERVICE BY HALF-VOLLEY:

(i) Using BACKHAND, HALF-VOLLEY TOUCH, return safely 10 Services, varied as to Topspin and Chop.

(ii) As (i) but using FOREHAND HALF-VOLLEY TOUCH.

Errors allowed: 5 (for 20 successes).

(b) COMBINING DRIVE-and-PUSH, FOREHAND:
Return 40 balls, which have been alternately pushed and chopped by using (respectively) TOPSPIN DRIVES AND PUSH-SHOTS, played alternately, Forehand, on one diagonal line.

Errors allowed: 5.

(c) COMBINING DRIVE-and-PUSH, BACKHAND:
As (b) but using BACKHAND throughout.

Errors allowed: 5.

(d) COMBINING (CHOPPED) DEFENSIVE RETURNS WITH PUSH, FOREHAND:
Return 40 balls, which have been alternately driven and

pushed, on same line, by using, respectively BACKSPIN DEFENSIVE RETURNS, and PUSHES, played alternately, on same line, all FOREHAND.

Errors allowed: 5.

(e) COMBINING (CHOPPED) DEFENSIVE RETURNS WITH PUSH, BACKHAND:

As (d) but using BACKHAND throughout.

Errors allowed: 5.

(f) LAWS, RULES, etc.

Answer 10 'everyday' questions on Laws and match procedure. Points allowed: For complete answer 3; for correct 'sense' 2; for part answer 1. 'Pass' score: 22 out of 30.

(g) MAINTAINING ATTACK AGAINST TOPSPIN FROM CONTROLLER:

(i) Maintain 10 triple sequences thus: 2 FOREHAND DRIVES plus 1 BACKHAND BLOCK.
Errors allowed: 4.

(ii) As (i) but sequences of 2 BACKHAND DRIVES plus 1 FOREHAND BLOCK.
Errors allowed: 4.

GOLD AWARD TESTS

Preliminary: Candidate must have passed the 'Silver' Tests. Candidate must pass six out of eight Tests attempted.

(a) TOPSPIN DRIVING UNDER PRESSURE, FOREHAND:

Play 50 FOREHAND TOPSPIN DRIVES, to one point, against Half-Volley returns which have been placed alternately to Areas 'C' and 'D'. Good Forehand position and footwork required throughout.

Errors allowed: 4.

(b) TOPSPIN DRIVING UNDER PRESSURE, BACKHAND:
As (a) but using BACKHAND TOPSPIN DRIVES.
Errors allowed: 4.

(c) COUNTER-DRIVING, CLOSE AND DISTANT, FOREHAND:
Return 20 Counter-Drives by means of FOREHAND COUNTER-DRIVES in sequences of 2 thus: 2 'Close', 2 'Distant', 2 'Close', etc, all returns kept on the same line.
Errors allowed: 2.

(d) COUNTER-DRIVING, CLOSE AND DISTANT . . . BACKHAND:
As (c), but using BACKHAND COUNTER-DRIVE.
Errors allowed: 2.

(e) COMBINING FOREHAND AND BACKHAND TOP-SPIN DRIVES:
Against slow chopped returns, which have been placed alternately to Area 'J' and 'K', by playing 20 FOREHAND AND BACKHAND TOPSPIN DRIVES, alternately, directed diagonally to Area 'F' and 'G'.
Errors allowed: 2.

(f) COMBINING FOREHAND AND BACKHAND DEFENSIVE BACKSPIN RETURNS:
Return 20 Drives, received alternately on Corner Areas 'J' and 'K', by means of, respectively FOREHAND AND BACKHAND CHOPPED RETURNS, to Area 'L'.
Errors allowed: 2.

(g) SEQUENCES OF TOPSPIN-AND-BACKSPIN STROKES:
Play 15 double sequences of FOREHAND CHOP AND BACKHAND DRIVE against balls which have been respectively Driven to the Forehand and Pushed to Backhand.
Errors allowed: 3 (total 30 balls).

(h) SEQUENCES OF TOPSPIN-AND-BACKSPIN STROKES:
Play the reverse of (g), (i.e. 'Backhand' for 'Forehand' and vice versa).
Errors allowed: 3 (total 30 balls).

(i) BACKHAND ATTACK 'DISTRIBUTION':
Play 10 triple sequences thus: DROPSHOT to Area 'E'; BACKHAND DRIVE to Area 'F'; BACKHAND DRIVE to Area 'G'; and repeat etc. Controller returns all balls to Area 'H'.
Errors allowed: 3.

(j) LOOP-TOPSPIN FOREHAND:
Candidate to demonstrate LOOP DRIVE 5 times, by either bouncing the ball to his own convenience, or requesting chopped returns of suitable length and strength, to suit his requirements. The aim is to show understanding of the 'loop' technique, and a continuity of loop drives is not demanded.

NOTES REGARDING ASSESSMENT

1. Candidates should be allowed to warm-up.
2. If only one item of a Test has been failed, a second attempt may be made the same day. If two items are failed, or one failed twice, a new application must be made for a re-Test. A re-Test may not be granted within one month of the failed Test.
3. 'Bronze' and 'Silver' may be taken on the same occasion, but only an ETTA-approved Assessor may make Silver Awards.
4. Assessors are responsible for arranging (a) Suitable Controllers to give each Candidate a fair chance, and (b) a Scorer, to keep count of 'successes' and 'errors'.
5. The 'Controller' should be a player able to place slow and steady balls to required targets, with required spin. Mis-

stakes by the Controller, or unlucky balls which are not appropriate to the required Test skill, will NOT be counted against the Candidate.

6. Assessors will rule on quality of performance appropriate to each Test level. A warning and explanation should be given to any Candidate who does not appear to have understood the precise requirements of any Test. A 'Push Shot' is a return which is low, slow, and straight, with a trace of Backspin.

7. Appropriate Target Areas are shown in the diagram (p. 154). Since the aim of Proficiency Awards is to train players to maintain control of Length and Direction, the Assessor should require good consistency in these respects, but allow for difficulties caused by inconsistent 'feeding' from the Controller, or difficult playing conditions. If the exchanges become difficult it is fairer to call a 'let', and re-start from the score already reached.

8. Marking of the Table: A, B, C, D, are Centre Points of the four 'Courts'. 'Target Areas' may be regarded as a 'notional' 18″ square. They need not be marked out in full; the red markers in our diagram provide, for practical purposes, a sufficient check on the length- and directional-control of the returns.

   Note: Two sheets of foolscap paper can form a useful approximation of these 'Centre Areas' when rehearsing the tests.

9. Assessors should inform Candidates of their decisions and notify results to the Organiser whose address appears on the blue Application Forms. (No. 6811.)

10. Bronze Award may be assessed by: Teachers; League Officials; ETTA Coaches or Students.

11. Silver Award may be assessed by ETTA Coaches, or by Players or Teachers approved for this task.

12. Gold Award will only be assessed at formal sessions organised by ETTA.

"TARGET" AREAS

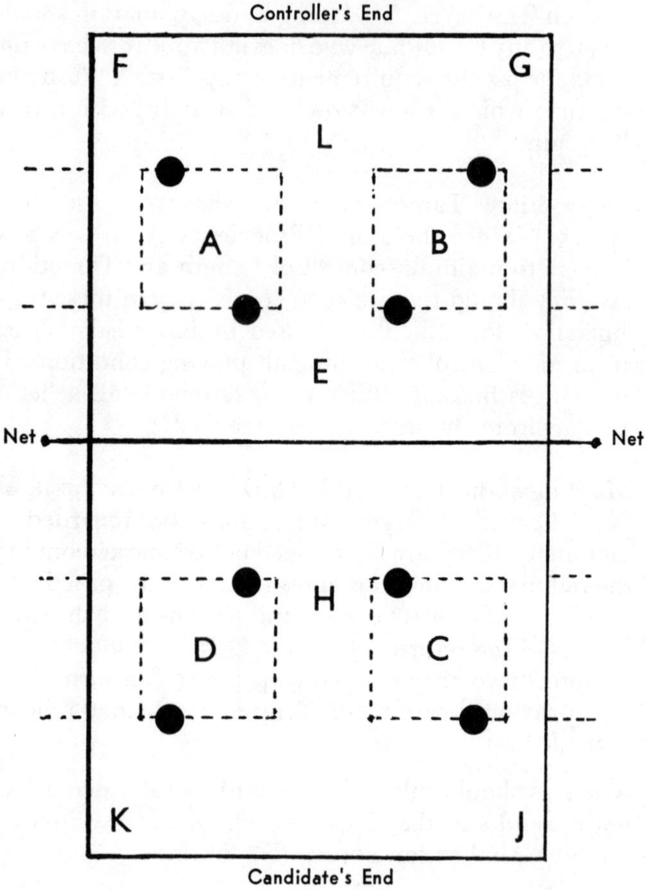

Controller's End

F

G

L

A

B

E

Net

Net

H

D

C

K

J

Candidate's End

Appendix Three **RECORDS**

WORLD CHAMPIONSHIPS

Team Events

Season and Venue		*Swaythling Cup (Men)*	*Corbillon Cup (Women)*
1926–7	London	Hungary	—
1927–8	Stockholm	,,	—
1928–9	Budapest	,,	—
1929–30	Berlin	,,	—
1930–1	Budapest	,,	—
1931–2	Prague	Czechoslovakia	—
1932–3	Baden (nr. Vienna)	Hungary	—
1933–4	Paris	,,	Germany
1934–5	London	,,	Czechoslovakia
1935–6	Prague	Austria	,,
1936–7	Baden	USA	USA
1937–8	London	Hungary	Czechoslovakia
1938–9	Cairo	Czechoslovakia	Germany
1946–7	Paris	,,	England
1947–8	London	,,	,,
1948–9	Stockholm	Hungary	USA
1949–50	Budapest	Czechoslovakia	Rumania
1950–1	Vienna	,,	,,
1951–2	Bombay	Hungary	Japan
1952–3	Bucharest	England	Rumania
1953–4	London	Japan	Japan
1954–5	Utrecht	,,	Rumania
1955–6	Tokyo	,,	,,
1956–7	Stockholm	,,	Japan
1958–9	Dortmund	,,	,,
1960–1	Peking	China	,,
1962–3	Prague	,,	,,
1964–5	Ljubljana	,,	China
1966–7	Stockholm	Japan	Japan
1968–9	Munich	,,	USSR
1970–1	Nagoya	China	Japan

Individual Events

Season	*Men's Singles*	*Men's Doubles*	*Women's Singles*	*Women's Doubles*	*Mixed Doubles*
1926–7	Dr R. Jacobi	Dr R. Jacobi & Dr D. Pecsi	M. Mednyanszky	M. Mednyanszky & F. Flamm	Z. Mechlovits & M. Mednyanszky
1927–8	Z. Mechlovits	A. Liebster & R. Thum	,,	,,	,,
1928–9	F. J. Perry	G. V. Barna & M. Szabados	,,	E. Metzger & Muller Ruster	I. Kelen & A. Sipos
1929–30	G. V. Barna	,,	,,	M. Mednyanszky & A. Sipos	M. Szabados & M. Mednyanszky
1930–1	M. Szabados	,,	,,	,,	,,
1931–2	G. V. Barna	,,	A. Sipos	,,	G. V. Barna & A. Sipos
1932–3	,,	G. V. Barna & S. Glancz	,,	,,	I. Kelen & M. Mednyanszky
1933–4	,,	G. V. Barna & M. Szabados	M. Kettnerova	,,	M. Szabados & M. Mednyanszky
1934–5	,,	,,	,,	,,	G. V. Barna & A. Sipos
1935–6	S. Kolar	R. H. Blattner & J. H. McClure	R. H. Aarons	M. Kettnerova & M. Smidova	M. Hamr & G. Kleinova
1936–7	R. Bergmann	,,	VACANT	V. Depetrisova & V. Votrubcova	B. Vana & V. Votrubcova

Season	*Men's Singles*	*Men's Doubles*	*Women's Singles*	*Women's Doubles*	*Mixed Doubles*
1937–8	B. Vana	S. Schiff & J. H. McClure	T. Pritzi	,,	L. Bellak & W. Woodhead
1938–9	R. Bergmann	G. V. Barna & R. Bergmann	V. Depetrisova	T. Pritzi & H. Bussmann	B. Vana & V. Votrubcova
1946–7	B. Vana	B. Vana & A. Slar	G. Farkas	G. Farkas & T. Pritzi	S. Soos & G. Farkas
1947–8	R. Bergmann	B. Vana & L. Stipeck	,,	Mrs V. Thomas & Miss P. Franks	R. Miles & T. Thall
1948–9	J. Leach	F. Tokar & I. Andreadis	,,	H. Elliot & G. Farkas	F. Sido & G. Farkas
1949–50	R. Bergmann	F. Sido & F. Soos	A. Rozeanu	D. Bergi & H. Elliot	F. Sido & G. Farkas
1950–1	J. Leach	B. Vana & I. Andreadis	,,	D. Rowe & R. Rowe	B. Vana & A. Rozeanu
1951–2	H. Satoh	N. Fujii & T. Hayashi	,,	S. Narahara & T. Nishimura	F. Sido & A. Rozeanu
1952–3	F. Sido	J. Koczian & F. Sido	,,	G. Farkas & A. Rozeanu	F. Sido & A. Rozeanu
1953–4	I. Ogimura	V. Harangozo & Z. Dolinar	,,	D. Rowe & R. Rowe	I. Andreadis & G. Farkas
1954–5	T. Tanaka	I. Andreadis & L. Stipek	,,	A. Rozeanu & E. Zeller	K. Szepesi & E. Doczian

Season	*Men's Singles*	*Men's Doubles*	*Women's Singles*	*Women's Doubles*	*Mixed Doubles*
1955–6	I. Ogimura	I. Ogimura & Y. Tomita	Miss T. Okawa	,,	E. Klein & Mrs L. Neuberger
1956–7	T. Tanaka	I. Andreadis & L. Stipek	Miss F. Eguchi	L. Moscoczy & A. Simon	I. Ogimura & F. Eguchi
1958–9	Jung Kuo-Tuan	I. Ogimura & T. Mrakami	Miss K. Matsu-zaki	T. Mamba & K. Yamaizumi	,,
1960–1	Chuang-Tse-Tung	N. Hishino & K. Kimura	Chiu Chung Hui	M. Alexandru & G. Pitica	I. Ogimura & K. Matsuzaki
1962–3	,,	Chuang Shim-Lin & Wang Chin-Liang	K. Matsuzaki	M. Matsuzaki & M. Seki	K. Kimura & K. Ito
1964–5	,,	Chuang-Tse-Tung & Hsu Yin-Sheng	N. Fukazu	Lin Hui-Ching & Cheng Min-Chin	K. Kimura & M. Seki
1966–7	N. Hasegawa	H. Alser & K. Johansson	S. Morisawa	S. Morisawa & S. Hirota	N. Hasegawa & N. Yamanaka
1968–9	S. Ito	,,	T. Kowada	S. Grinberg & Z. Rudnova	N. Hasegawa & Y. Konno
1970–1	S. Bengtsson	I. Jonyer & T. Klampar	Lin Hui-Ching	Lin Hui-Ching & Cheng Min-Chin	Chang Sin-Lin & Lin Hui-Ching

EUROPEAN CHAMPIONSHIPS

Team Events

Season and Venue		*Hungary Cup (Men)*	*Rumania Cup (Women)*
1957–8	Budapest	Hungary	England
1959–60	Zagreb	Hungary	Hungary
1961–2	West Berlin	Yugoslavia	Germany (DTTB)
1963–4	Malmo	Sweden	England
1965–6	London	,,	Hungary
1967–8	Lyons	,,	Germany (DTTB)
1969–70	Moscow	,,	—

EUROPEAN CHAMPIONSHIPS

Individual Events

Season	*Men's Singles*	*Men's Doubles*	*Women's Singles*	*Women's Doubles*	*Mixed Doubles*
1957–8	Z. Berczik	L. Stipek & L. Vyhnanobsky	E. Koczian	A. Rozeanu & E. Zeller	Z. Berczik & G. Farkas
1959–60	,,	Z. Berczik & F. Sido	,,	A. Rozeanu & M. Alexandru	G. Corbirzan & M. Alexandru
1961–2	H. Alser	V. Markovic & J. Teran	Mrs A. Simon	D. Rowe & M. Shannon	H. Alser & Mrs I. Harst
1963–4	K. Johansson	J. Stanek & V. Miko	E. Koczian	,,	P. Rozsas & S. Lukacs
1965–6	,,	K. Johansson & H. Alser	Mrs M. Zlexan-dru	E. Koczian & E. Jurik	V. Miko & M. Luzova
1967–8	D. Surbek	A. Stipancic & E. Vecko	Miss I. Vostova	J. Karlikova & M. Luzova	S. Gomoskov & Z. Rudnova
1969–70	H. Alser	A. Stipancic & D. Surbek	Z. Rudnova	Z. Rudnova & Grinberg	,,